Knowledge, Belief,
and Witchcraft

Mestizo Spaces
Espaces Métissés

V. Y. Mudimbe
EDITOR

Bogumil Jewsiewicki
ASSOCIATE EDITOR

Knowledge, Belief, and Witchcraft

Analytic Experiments in African Philosophy

Barry Hallen and J. Olubi Sodipo
With a New Foreword by W.V.O. Quine
and a New Afterword by Barry Hallen

STANFORD UNIVERSITY PRESS
STANFORD, CALIFORNIA 1997

Stanford University Press
Stanford, California

First published in 1986 by Ethnographica, Ltd.
© 1986 Barry Hallen and J.O. Sodipo
Foreword © 1986 Dorothy Emmet

New Foreword and Afterword
© 1997 by the Board of Trustees
of the Leland Stanford Junior University

Printed in the United States of America

CIP data appear at the end of the book

To our parents
and
to the Adahunse of Ijan-Ekiti

Acknowledgements

A large number of people contributed to the completion of the earlier edition of this book. Unfortunately, as we explain in the Introduction, we are prohibited from mentioning many of them by name. Of the many we can name, the first and foremost remains Olufemi L. Osatuyi, who for years worked as the Chief Research Assistant to the project, and did so in an extremely diligent and responsible manner. Dorothy Emmet provided constant support and inspiration for the project from the very beginning and was kind enough to comment on the original manuscript in detail. Robin Horton was also a source of encouragement and a valued commentator. W.V.O. Quine was kind enough to comment on the first two chapters and to correct some misrepresentations of the indeterminacy thesis, and graciously agreed to contribute a Foreword to the new edition. Finally, we should like to express our profound gratitude to the Onijan of Ijan-Ekiti, Oba J.A. Obarinde, whose hospitality, friendship, and support were indispensable to the successful completion of the project.

Among others whose comments, advice, and support have been helpful are Rowland Abiodun, Kayode Adetugbo, Robert G. Armstrong, Karin Barber, Carla De Benedetti, E.A. Caxton-Martins, Carolyne Dennis, 'Lola Durojaiye, Elizabeth Eames, Donna Finan, Bill Haigh, Roger Makanjuola, Ian Malpass, Michael Martin, Margaret Masterman, Valentin Mudimbe, Keith Nicklin, 'Segun Osoba, Susan Staniland, 'Funmi Faniran Togonu-Bickersteth, Pierre Verger, Helen Verran, Kwasi Wiredu, and our colleagues in the Department of Philosophy, Obafemi Awolowo University (formerly the University of Ife), Nigeria. Our thanks as well to the Central Research Committees of the University of Lagos and the University of Ife for their generous support. Helen Tartar and Pamela MacFarland Holway of Stanford University Press have made everything having to do with getting this text into print easier than it ever was before. Last, but far from least, thanks to the Director, Fellows, and staff of the W.E.B. Du Bois Institute, Harvard University, for their fraternity and support.

Contents

Foreword to the American Edition

This book is philosophical and linguistic, serving both interests. On the philosophical side it embodies the spirit of the philosophy of ordinary language, which flourished in England in the middle decades of this century; but the language concerned, Yoruba, is far from ordinary from an English point of view.

The central epistemological themes of truth, belief, knowledge, and evidence are explored through analytic study of the usage and connotation of the key terms: not these four words, to be sure, but the accepted dictionary counterparts in Yoruba. One's linguistic interest is aroused and nourished by the divergences in usage that emerge between the Yoruba terms and their canonical translations, under the expert interrogation of thoughtful natives by our two philosophically sophisticated authors.

Hints of an alien philosophical orientation emerge, which one might hope to articulate and integrate into a coherent and novel philosophical attitude. This could enrich one's own attitude with a new perspective. Meanwhile, this study strikingly exposes the Procrustean measures to which one is driven, for practical purposes, in translating abstract terms from remote languages.

W.V.O. Quine
October 1995

Preface to the American Edition

It is gratifying to learn that, ten years after its first publication, there is sufficient interest in *KBW* (to use the acronym with which this little book has come to be identified) to warrant this new edition. That the book can still be of interest is in no small part due to the greater variety of intellectual and cultural currents active in contemporary academia. The combined onslaughts of the postcolonial, the multicultural, and the postmodern are tailor-made for a text that proposes to introduce readers to elements of an alternative cognitive system—an alternative way to understand and explain the world and human experience.

KBW did not set out to be a 'radical' text. If anything, its aim was orthodoxy—to apply techniques derived from mainstream linguistic philosophy to a non-Western language. It is perhaps because this kind of crossing of cultures by analytic philosophy has rarely been undertaken in a systematic manner that some of our findings have provoked controversy.

Why had this not happened earlier? Why has it taken so long for academic philosophy to become directly involved with the cognitive systems of non-Western cultures? If the explanation is that the cultures of sub-Saharan Africa were assigned so low a ranking on the cross-cultural index of rationality that they were not thought to warrant serious interest on the part of philosophers, our response would be that, at the least, philosophers themselves should have queried and tested this erroneous generalization. *KBW* does set out to test it, and to argue that it is either false or overstated, a product of those who fail to appreciate that there may indeed be more than one road to the 'truth'.

One of the broader points of *KBW* therefore becomes that philosophers should reclaim their right to study and to define the rational in any culture in the world today. That this controversially experimental claim has since been correctly interpreted and enlarged upon by mainstream colleagues is reassuring. The Foreword to this new edition by Professor Quine, as well as his comments on the original text, attests to this remarkable philosopher's early appreciation of our intentions.

Mention should be made of a few more specific points. Although we should have liked to edit out all instances of gendered pronouns, considerations of time and expense have not made this possible. It is therefore important to note here that in the Yoruba language pronouns are *not* gendered. The same word is used regardless of whether the person being referred to happens to be female or male. Gendering was introduced in the process of translating the original Yoruba into English, a language in which pronouns *are* gendered. We hope readers will appreciate, moreover, that when this text was originally crafted gender-specific language was not a point at issue.

Several commentators have challenged our presentations of Yoruba meanings as if they were timeless and unchanging. That was never our intention. The meanings recorded and analyzed here were conventional in the Ekiti region during the period between 1974 and 1984. From a philosophical vantage point, whenever in history they happened to be used does not in the least detract from their interest as rendering alternative notions of cognition.

The present edition contains as an Afterword a paper by Barry Hallen detailing the philosophical overview and methodology underlying this text's conception. Less effort was originally directed towards describing this aspect of the project because of our conviction at the time that there needed to be less talk about '*how* to do' philosophy in Africa and more energy devoted simply to '*doing*' philosophy in and of Africa. In addition, the Bibliography has been revised and updated so as to include a fairly wide sampling of works that are relevant to the possibility of non-Western cognitive alternatives, as well as publications that discuss *KBW*, whether in critical or positive terms.

Barry Hallen
W.E.B. Du Bois Institute
Harvard University

Knowledge, Belief, and Witchcraft

Foreword

I first met Dr Barry Hallen in 1974, when I was a consultant at the University of Ibadan in Nigeria, advising on the setting up of a Department of Philosophy. I had approached this assignment with a number of unresolved questions in mind. I had no doubt that any university should have a Department of Philosophy, but what kind of courses should it offer? I had already acted for three years as external examiner in philosophy in the University of Ife, where J.O. Sodipo was head of the department. I had become aware of the intellectual sterility that can set in when students reproduce by rote learning the views of Western philosophers without seeing the problems behind them, and, worse still, without appreciating that these might also be their own problems. Professor Sodipo was well aware of this, and he was involved in starting and editing the journal *Second Order*, which was designed to provide a forum for serious discussion of philosophy in an African context. He had already worked hard and successfully to build up a good department of philosophy at Ife, and to encourage an analytic and critical approach to the discipline.

I felt that there was a need for philosophers, whether African or expatriate, who were both competent in Western philosophy and had entered deeply into a traditional African belief system, who could see how similar problems might arise in the different contexts. These might then be able to help students from a traditional background to appreciate what the problems were, to articulate their own approach, and to compare it with the approaches of Western philosophers. I thought that the kinds of problems which might be treated in this way would be likely to be in ethics, political philosophy, and the philosophical psychology of the human person – I don't think I had sufficiently seen that they might be epistemological problems.

The philosopher I found in Nigeria who saw things in a similar way was Barry Hallen, then at the University of Lagos. He was realistically aware of how much work would need to be done. One must live for a considerable time in a local community, and get the confidence of the custodians of the traditional beliefs. In the case of the Yoruba, these were the *babaláwo* ('fathers of secrets') and the *oníṣègùn* ('masters of medicine'). He was able to move to the University of Ife, and undertake just such a long term project in Ekiti with Professor Sodipo's participation, encouragement and support.

Since then I have had continued contacts with Barry Hallen, both on subsequent visits to Nigeria and on his visits to England, and I have followed what he has been doing with admiration. In particular I have been impressed by how he was able to establish a colleague relationship with his informants, so that they could pursue themes of mutual interest in unhurried conversations. This book is the first – but we can hope by no means the last – outcome of the work. It leads in with a fairly long discussion of Professor Quine's thesis about the 'indeterminacy of translation'. This was the contention that a number of different theoretical statements, 'standing sentences', can interpret the same ostensibly factual material, and that even where the same concepts are used their meaning can vary in different contexts. This has the still stronger implication that the use of an abstract term in one language may not be the same as that of the term taken to translate it in another. There is thus a philosophical and not only a linguistic problem over the translation of such terms and this needs to be grasped by those who try to present an alien belief system in another language. The authors of this book grasp it tightly, and they test the thesis of indeterminacy of translation by examining the uses of the words *mọ̀* and *gbàgbọ́* to see whether their usual translation as 'know' and 'believe' can be accepted unequivocably. In doing this they find they go some of the way with Quine's thesis, but do not need to go all the way into scepticism over the possibility of translation of abstract concepts. Furthermore, their examination of the uses of *mọ̀* and *gbàgbọ́* bring out what might be called a Yoruba epistemology more sophisticated than is generally acknowledged in anthropological literature. Here the dominant view has been that 'knowledge' in traditional societies is something given through oral tradition and accepted as authoritative. Our authors claim, on the basis of their protracted discussions, that this is too simple a view. Oral tradition is second hand information which gives things 'one agrees to accept' – this is a better translation of *gbàgbọ́* than is 'belief'. But *mọ̀* – knowledge – is something one knows at first hand, notably from sensory evidence. So tracing out these usages shows how a 'second order' concern with the meanings of words can have direct relevance to a 'first order' anthropological view. The study of usages of these particular words shows the Yoruba *onísègùn* are more sophisticated epistemologically, and more critically, and indeed empirically, minded than has been generally supposed.

This has implications, not only for anthropologists, but in the very alive controversy over what constitutes 'African Philosophy'. Here there are two dominant views: on the one hand, a somewhat romantic and at times politically motivated, presentation of what is said to have been the pristine African world view before it was contaminated by Western influences. On the other hand, it is maintained that philosophy should be purely critical and analytic, and, as this quality is absent in the traditional views, philosophy as taught by and to Africans should be something entirely distinct from 'African Philosophy'. 'African Philosophy' has perhaps been more in evidence in Francophone than in Anglophone circles. In the former there was a strong influence from P. Tempels's *La philosophie bantou*. This presented the African world view as life lived in a locally ordered hierarchical community that was also a manifestation of a world which was a total organic community, pervaded by living forces. This outlook was handed down in oral tradition, and educated Africans needed to recover and assert it against the 'scientific materialism' of the West. This programme was promoted in the journal *Présence Africaine*, whose contributors included gifted writers such as Senghor and Césaire. The latter coined the term *négritude* for this outlook. The reaction against *négritude* is under way. It was challenged politically as leading Africans into a romantic dream of their own past, and distracting them from realistic political struggles. Wole Soyinka gave it a *coup de grâce* by remarking that when a tiger is attacked it attacks back, and does not talk about its 'tigritude'. Theoretically, it has been attacked by philosophers such as K. Wiredu, P. Bodunrin, and most recently, P.J. Hountondji in his book *African Philosophy: Myth and Reality* (Hutchinson, 1983). These all see philosophy as critical thinking, and fear that the promotion of 'African Philosophy' can hinder African students from acquiring the necessary intellectual tools. In the matter of views not of philosophy but of fact, they question what Hountondji calls 'unanimism', the notion that there is a universal African world view. Doubt is also thrown on this by Dr Hallen's researches. The last chapter, dealing with witchcraft, shows evidence that witchcraft is not a phenomenon with certain constant features, as has been supposed. This chapter is thus not only an essay on a particular topic, but an illustration of a general theoretical point. Moreover, the discussions reported throughout the book show that the notion that Africans are not capable of critical thinking is manifestly untrue, not only of the educated, but also of these *oníṣègùn*.

If the remarks these make show that they are not only shrewd, but can be empirically minded, this has a bearing on the controversy among anthropologists as to the correct way of taking traditional views about matters such as spirits and occult powers. The dominant view among anthropologists has been the 'symbolist' one: these views do not express propositions purporting to be true about the world, but they are symbolic ways of expressing attitudes which can give practical direction or strengthen morale in social situations, especially those of crisis, conflict, or disaster. This, of course, is an onlooker's interpretation, not that of the participants themselves, who surely believe that they are stating factual truths. The alternative, called, perhaps not very happily, the 'intellectualist' view, is to accept that these must be taken seriously as assertions of how people believe the world is. Robin Horton has been the best known exponent of this interpretation, and he has put it in a form that bears directly on the controversy over 'African Philosophy'. Horton says that, while making assertions about the world, these traditional views are 'closed', in that they are not laid open to criticism, empirical testing, and revision, and that they must therefore be contrasted with scientific views which are held critically and are always corrigible by further evidence. His work has generated considerable controversy, some of which went on in the journal *Second Order*. If he is right, not only over a good deal of traditional belief, but in a generalization across its whole spectrum, this would sharpen the contrast between so-called 'African Philosophy' and critical thought. But if Hallen and Sodipo are right in detecting sceptical and indeed empirical elements in their informants' view of *mọ̀*, 'knowledge', and its distinction from *gbàgbọ́*, what one 'agrees to accept', this bears importantly on how far the distinction is an absolute one.

The right note in considering 'African Philosophy', or, better, philosophy in Africa, was struck, I think, by Wiredu. (See, for example, some of the papers in his *Philosophy and an African Culture*, (C.U.P., 1980), especially 'On an African Orientation in Philosophy' and 'How not to compare African traditional thought with Western thought'). He says that Western critical philosophy developed out of a background of what he calls 'folk philosophy', namely that of the ancient Greeks and Hebrews. Why should not capacities to do critical philosophy be developed in people starting from another kind of folk philosophy? To ignore this background can produce a split in the minds of those who are now getting a largely Western-type education but who also need to come to terms with their traditional beliefs. In talking to our African colleagues (and to Dr Hallen and Professor Sodipo they are indeed colleagues), we can be aware that this is also our problem in coming to terms with our own Judaeo-Christian and Hellenic heritage.

A shared concern to elicit folk philosophy can lead to a rich kind of discussion, but it depends on being able to find appropriate concepts and on not imposing alien ones. Those of us who would like to be able to carry on such discussions, but have neither the opportunities for prolonged stay nor the knowledge of the languages, will find that this book provides highly valuable material.

DOROTHY EMMET
CAMBRIDGE, 1985

Introduction

1. The Disrepute of African Philosophy

One of the more challenging conditions of working in the general area of cross-cultural studies is that the divisions between different disciplines are less rigorously observed. This is more because of a growing awareness that psychological, philosophical, sociological, and even medical considerations may be interrelated or relevant to one another, than to an opinion that cross-cultural studies are still in their infancy, or that in relatively 'underdeveloped' cultures such special interest divisions have yet to be consciously established. In what follows we hope to make some cross-cultural and inter-disciplinary comparisons between Western culture and a particular African culture which the existent literature often refers to as 'traditional' in character.

In whatever way the domain of African philosophy may ultimately be delimited, increasing controversy is being generated by the phrase 'African *traditional* systems of thought' and the role they are to play in it. There are those who argue that traditional systems of thought are of marginal philosophical interest because of the lack of emphasis they place upon critical or reflective thinking. The sense of the word 'traditional' is that the reasons or explanations most commonly produced by such thought systems are little more than an appeal *to* tradition ('We know this is the case because the forefathers said so.'). Some therefore go so far as to argue that African philosophy in any true sense of the term began relatively recently, with a generation of African intellectuals who have deliberately chosen to transcend tradition, and who have undergone professional training in the methods of contemporary academic philosophy. The philosophical issues or problems (including that of a comparative lack of critical thinking in these belief systems) that such philosophers choose to concern themselves with may be of particular relevance to African societies, but the methodologies with which they analyse and attempt to solve them – the methodologies of contemporary academic philosophy (language analysis, Marxism, phenomenology, etc.) – are trans-cultural.

Others reject use of the word 'traditional' altogether. The word 'traditional' is pejorative if used to imply that some peoples' intellectual abilities have yet to become 'modern,' to become rigorously critical and systematic. This may indeed be true of many people in any African culture, but it is no less true of many people in any other culture (including the so-called 'developed' countries), thereby rendering use of the word redundant.

Whatever the outcome may eventually be, this controversy over the appropriateness of the word 'traditional' is indicative of a real problem that should be recognized by anyone who has some interest in African philosophy. Philosophy today has become, almost exclusively, an academic endeavour. But African philosophy, in order to be at least infused by the (oral) knowledge, beliefs and values of African cultures, needs to establish and maintain links with African society-at-large outside the university. And it is over this business of going outside the university community into African society that the philosopher must professionally come to terms with another of his academic colleagues, the social anthropologist.

Social anthropology too deserves part of the credit for the interdisciplinary nature of African studies. The social anthropologist believes that it is necessary to have some understanding of all of a culture's institutions before one is entitled to write a knowledgeable account of it. But in Africa particularly, social anthropology is today under suspicion because it, more than any other discipline, is held responsible for introducing the word 'traditional' (as a replacement for the even more pejorative 'primitive') as descriptive of African cultures and systems of thought.

To date it is anthropologists who have been professionally trained to undertake fieldwork in African communities of the sort required to make systematic studies of African systems of thought. And it is the writings of anthropologists that are primarily responsible for the image of African systems of thought as of little serious philosophical interest. Africans believe in the sorts of things they do because they are *not* scientific, because they have *no* written records, because they *fail* to make an adequate distinction between the rational and the emotional, and so forth. They are said to manifest and to 'know' world-views, which are akin to collections of mythical or religious beliefs about the nature of reality.

The influence of this picture of African thought systems has been profound and, for our purposes, has had two important consequences. Firstly, it has persuaded many philosophers (including a number who are themselves African) that the wisdom of African societies is something better left to the domains of anthropology and religion, and that 'traditional' African philosophy is not therefore an area of specialization in which they are keen to develop a facility. Secondly, even if courses in this African pseudo-philosophy have managed to gain a place in some departments of philosophy, this is explained away as due primarily to certain contemporary social, political and historical conditions rather than to the intrinsic merit of the subject-matter.

2. *Methodologies for African Philosophy*

The methodologies for presenting African philosophy are as many as the above variety of opinions implies. Some, the so-called ethno-philosophers or ethnographers with some philosophical background, argue that African philosophy should consist of *descriptions* of African beliefs on topics of philosophical relevance: death, good behaviour, the supreme deity, and so forth. Others argue that African philosophy should consist of what Africans who are professionally trained as academic philosophers produce. If the majority today happen to be concerned with social philosophy, this is a reflection of the needs they are being asked to fulfil by their societies, rather than a reason to denigrate African philosophy as too narrow or ideologically motivated.

* * *

When we first concentrated our interests upon the field of African philosophy we too found the existent, printed (ethnophilosophical) sources unsatisfactory, but it was not clear whether the reasons for this were due to the nature of the beliefs of the African peoples from whom they had been drawn or to the methodologies of the collectors. For if a collector begins his work already committed to the view that the beliefs are held on a non-critical and non-reflective basis, one could hardly expect him to be sensitive to evidence to the contrary.

With social anthropology we felt that the problem was somewhat different. The interest of this profession in the abstract thought of 'traditional' peoples developed in relatively recent times. Previously social anthropologists had tended to concentrate on a society's social *institutions* and how they, for example, contributed to its welfare and betterment. But when special attention was directed to what such peoples themselves claimed to know and how they claimed to be able to demonstrate their knowledge, the majority of the fieldworkers opted for the position that has variously come to be known as poetic-symbolism, expressionism, or emotivism. It maintains that much of the so-called knowledge of traditional cultures is magical in nature – symbolic or expressive of what their peoples would like to accomplish but which, without substantive scientific development, they are in fact unable to do. But they derive at least some relief from (ritual) *beliefs* that tell them they are able to do something, regardless of however ultimately ineffective, when confronted by a problem.

Symbolism is by no means representative of all of social anthropology today. There are those mavericks who disagree with their colleagues in a forceful and eloquent fashion (Horton 1967). But because this is the (numerically) dominant position in the English-language tradition, researchers from other disciplines who are interested in an alternative approach to the abstract or theoretical thought of such cultures are often disappointed by what they find social anthropology has to say.

As academics with philosophical backgrounds who were interested in such an alternative methodological approach to the study of 'traditional' African thought, we found our task to be a daunting one. There appeared to be no existing suitable technique we could copy or imitate. In a series of exploratory and deliberately hypothetical articles we therefore undertook the piece-meal, gradual elaboration of a methodology that would require the academic philosopher to go outside the university confines and, as an equal, engage in *discussions* of philosophical import with his *colleagues* in African society. This single sentence alone has raised so many queries and objections that an account of and our responses to them should suffice as an introduction to our approach to African philosophy.

Since a project of this sort would evidently require some sort of fieldwork, whereby academic philosophers would go out into African societies and meet with their wise men and collect information, we were asked whether we had ever undergone any professional training about how to do this sort of thing. We were cautioned about the misrepresentations and excesses that may be engendered by leading questions, browbeating, and selective quotation.

We were asked to be more precise about what we meant by 'discussions'. Was the basis to be questionnaires which would 'lead' the conversation in certain directions? Were they to involve genuine *exchanges* of information to which, as the word 'discussion' implies, all parties would contribute equally? Or were we not in fact primarily out to pick the brains of our wise men in a manner very much akin to that of the ethnographer?

How and where would we find our wise men? Is someone who is knowledgeable or wise about, for example, agriculture thereby entitled to be regarded as a colleague by a university philosophy teacher? Is each wise man to be treated as an individual, potentially eccentric thinker, or are opinions to be somehow collated and presented as shared and communal?

And what of the relationship between the thoughts of the wise men and those of the more ordinary and average members of the community? Are the latter not to be taken into account and the former to be treated as their official intellectual interpreters and, if so, can any convincing justification or proof for this be given?

And, finally is it representative to refer to these wise men as our 'colleagues'? We might choose to regard them as such, but would they care to look upon us as *their* colleagues? They play a vital, active, and therefore different role in their societies, while the university and its academic 'doctors' represent a foreign, closed and ludicrously luxurious educational system whose avowed ideology, to some degree, is to be isolated from the society at large and to make few direct practical contributions to it.

These are important and serious questions, and frankly we cannot adequately answer them all. Nevertheless out of the story of the research project which we are about to tell we believe that we can provide answers to at least some and indicate a line of future research along which the answers to those remaining will lie.

* * *

Contact with a particular African society eventually grew out of a voluntary, non-credit, student study group on African philosophy first established in 1973 at the University of Lagos, Nigeria. Members of the group came from a variety of ethnic backgrounds from the south and middle-belt of Nigeria. One means for increasing communication between the university community and society at large was for the students to establish face-to-face fieldwork relationships with the elders and wise men of their family compounds, villages and towns, but the only occasions on which they were able to meet with these people were during the university vacations, which were relatively few and far between. Despite this limitation some progress was made once agreement had been reached about a topic for discussion. This had to be something that was of academic, philosophical relevance and which would also be meaningful to the elders and wise men. After lengthy discussions the topic chosen was the concept of the 'person'. Its limits were rather loosely defined, but they were understood to extend to such things as the various (physical and/or spiritual) parts of the person, the interrelations between them, the various types of persons or personalities, and the more important forces to which a person may be subject and which he may exercise.

The information that came back from a particular village, Ijan, in the Yoruba area of southwestern Nigeria known as Ekiti, was so stimulating that eventually the study group coordinator decided to concentrate exclusively upon that village and to establish a fully-fledged, university sponsored research project on the Yoruba concept of *'èniyàn'* (usually translated into English as 'person'). This was a fortunate choice, as one of the co-authors of this book is Yoruba and the other has spent his entire Nigerian university career in the Yoruba areas.

The majority of the persons in this village whom we chose to concern ourselves with are those the Yoruba refer to as *onísègùn*. In times past Europeans erroneously stigmatized them as 'witch doctors', but the name may be rendered literally as 'master of medicine'. In English they are also sometimes referred to as 'herbalists' or as 'native doctors'. We chose them for several reasons. The *onísègùn* represent and exercise a level of understanding and analysis of Yoruba life and thought that is more critically sophisticated than that of the ordinary person. In fact it is the ordinary person that they spend much of their time advising. And a comparable study of another suitable, knowledgeable group in Yoruba society, the *Ifá babaláwo*, was already well underway (Abimbola 1975; 1976; 1977).

As we wanted to relate to the *onísègùn* more as colleagues than as informants, data was collected in the context of guided, sometimes cross-cultural, discussions rather than in question and answer sessions. But it proved one thing to have such discussions, and quite another to put them into a form that would communicate itself to academic philosophers. We did not want to tell the 'story' of another world-view, as we have said before.

In 1975 the research project moved to the University of Ife, Nigeria. Still trying to find a way to present the discussions in a philosophically acceptable form, we flirted with phenomenology but found it a more difficult methodology to practise than to preach. This methodological quandary continued until the day, when reading through the English translations of some of the discussions, we noticed that certain Yoruba words had throughout unquestioningly been translated into English as 'true', 'false', 'know', 'believe', etc. As the philosophical criteria governing the usage of these English terms are often strictly defined, and as we had never bothered to make specific enquires about the criteria governing their supposed Yoruba equivalents, this seemed a wise comparison to undertake in order to discover whether our translations were justified. This enquiry led to the second chapter of this book.

In working out the comparison we have adopted a methodology that borrows heavily from the philosophical tradition known as conceptual analysis. Making reference to several standard philosophical works and a bit of common sense, we endeavour to summarize the conditions or criteria governing usage of 'know' and 'believe' in the English language. Making use of the examples, explanations, and analyses of the *oníṣẹ̀gùn*, we then endeavour to sum up the conditions or criteria governing their supposed Yoruba equivalents, '*mọ̀*' and '*gbàgbọ́*,' and finally to compare the two systems.

One point of controversy arising out of this chapter will be whether the *oníṣẹ̀gùn* are competent to undertake the kinds of linguistic analyses which will entitle them to be considered, in this regard, satisfactory equivalents of the academic philosopher. Are they competent to discuss the ordinary usage of theoretical concepts and are they cabable of reflecting upon and explaining such usage to a degree that exceeds that of the ordinary person? As we have made an effort to quote them directly whenever possible, we feel that the material serves as its own justification. Nevertheless, if it is even part of the professional task of the *oníṣẹ̀gùn* to offer his clients explanations that are connected to and yet exceed the ordinary, it is reasonable to expect that their understanding of the theoretical concepts involved will also be connected to and exceed the ordinary.

The academic philosopher is expected to produce a *systematic* account, whether of ordinary usage or his own alternative theory. Is the same to be found in the explanations of the *oníṣẹ̀gùn*? Our answer is a qualified 'yes'. Certainly the system revealed by their remarks is not as deliberately and therefore obviously structured as the epistemological theories of academic philosophy. Who would expect it to be? They are men of practice as well as theory. But by concentrating upon those passages in which structural relationships are clearly implied, and by carefully collating and comparing statements made by all the *oníṣẹ̀gùn* over the entire nine year period, we are reasonably confident that the end-product is representative of an important and provocative theoretical statement from the Yoruba conceptual system. No doubt it may be possible to provide other examples, derived from the conceptual system, that diverge from this outline. No language system is entirely consistent. Our general practice, we hope, has been to prefer the ordinary to the extraordinary.

3. *Translating Abstract Ideas and Translation Indeterminacy*

Philosophy is well-known for examining its presuppositions before it actually begins to argue for something. Often this is for the good, because the philosopher is therby made aware of things he is taking for granted that may cause trouble later on. Better to build a house on a sound foundation than to have it fall apart before completed. But sometimes people both in and outside of philosophy become frustrated and then bored by what they regard as excessive nit-picking, as an almost sick fascination with the anticipation of trivial objections before they have even been raised.

After outlining our proposed methodology in much the same form as in the preceding subsection, our attention was drawn to a presupposition underlying it that did seem to deserve some attention: the ease or difficulty of expressing the abstract or theoretical ideas of one culture in the language of another. Human beings generally presuppose that they all share certain feelings, states of mind, and experiences in common simply (somehow) by virtue of being human. The word for one of these basic states or experiences or things in one language may be spelled differently and sound differently from the word meaning the same thing in another language. This is part of the colourful cultural diversity of mankind. But what is more important is that the *meanings* of the two different words are the same. This is why we can construct bilingual dictionaries, learn one another's languages and, in short, communicate. We may occasionally encounter a rather bizarre word in a foreign language for which we can find no one-to-one equivalent. In this case we may have to write a short paragraph, a monograph, or even a whole book in order adequately to explain it. But the important thing is that we can explain it, and afterwards be confident that we have done so correctly.

Much of this commonsense approach to communication between cultures, and therefore to the possibilities of expressing the abstract ideas of an African culture in, for example, the English language (something our own metholodogy presumed it was possible to do), has been challenged by a contemporary analytic philosopher, W.V.O. Quine. Quine's argument, known as the *indeterminacy thesis of radical translation*, is therefore the subject of our first chapter. For if one is not able to be confident of expressing the meanings of one culture with the language of another, the entire edifice of cross-cultural studies and of African philsophy written in anything other than African languages is threatened.

So as not to misrepresent Quine and to make it seem as if the *practical* consequences of his argument are more momentous than he means them to be, we must constantly remind ourselves of the kind of argument he is making. Quine is arguing as a philosopher, as someone who *imagines* (he calls it a 'thought experiment') what the conditions governing a unique translation situation *might* be and the problems that *could* follow from them. He is not writing as a linguist, as a social anthropologist, or as a fieldworker because he never has been one. Therefore he cautions us in the strongest terms against taking the problems he does identify or the recommendations he does make as guidelines for the practising linguist or fieldworker.

Nevertheless, without erring to that extreme, without rewriting Quine's arguments into a field guide for linguists, it is still possible to derive certain practical precautions, sensitivities, and insights about language that may prevent (or at least curtail) semantic misrepresentations of other cultures. This is the point of the third chapter, in which we demonstrate that a basic confusion about the nature of language, of meaning, and of theory has produced a thoroughly muddled, but generally assumed theory of witchcraft, and a misrepresentation and misunderstanding of its supposed equivalent in Yoruba culture.

4. Before We Begin

The *oníṣègùn* with whom we are working are more than simply masters of medicine. Otherwise one could question their being assigned a knowledge status any higher than that of a master of agriculture or a master of weaving. Knowing medicine entails knowing the force and powers of the ingredients of a medicine, and knowing these entails knowing the forces and powers of the natural world in which they are found, of the spiritual realm that lies behind and engenders that natural world, and of the human beings by whom they are made and to whom many of them are applied. One therefore finds the *oníṣègùn* being asked to give advice and counsel about business dealings, family problems, unhappy personal situations, religious problems, and the future, as well as about physical and mental illness. Such a wide breadth of learning and experience entitles the best of them to be regarded as more than ordinary, even though they are exceedingly modest and maintain a deliberately low profile in the community.

But how is one to determine who among them are the best? In Ijan there are approximately forty full-fledged *oníṣègùn*, supplemented by perhaps another twenty people who have some partial knowledge of medicine that enables them to be of help with specific problems. Of the forty perhaps a dozen are regarded as men of exceptional ability. This is determined in two ways: by the villagers who are their clients and who carefully monitor and gauge the records of their successes and failures, and by their own professional colleagues. In the community the *oníṣègùn* comprise, and monitor their own activities by means of, an *ẹgbẹ́* or professional society. This society acts as the institutional guardian of the knowledge that is at the heart of the profession. It judges every individual member in terms of his competence and character. It reprimands and disciplines. It determines whether an individual has demonstrated that he is sufficiently responsible to advance, to be entrusted with greater knowledge and powers. And it invokes

13

the pledge of secrecy upon all its members to ensure that neither the knowledge nor powers of medicine should fall into non-professional or irresponsible hands.

Because of the above social and professional constraints, before the dozen or so with whom we are working would agree to enter into discussions with us there are certain conditions with which we have been asked to comply. The first is that we talk with them only on an individual basis (to a point where we are even discouraged from mentioning the name of one in the house of another). The second is that we never tell or repeat to one what we have learned from another. The third is that in anything we publish we must not reveal their names. If we violate any of these three conditions, their participation in the project will be subject to termination.

1. Indeterminacy and the Translation of Alien Behaviour

In the long run, however, an ethnographer is bound to triumph. Armed with preliminary knowledge nothing can prevent him from driving deeper and deeper the wedge if he is interested and persistent.

E.E. Evans-Pritchard (1937)

1. Introduction

Philosophers would regard the absolute terms with which Evans-Pritchard embraces cross-cultural understanding in the above quotation as unrealistic. Philsophy is interested, in particular, in abstract conceptual meanings. Concepts have often been found difficult to make clear (and define) within the language that uses them. English-language philosophers are consequently responsible for countless conflicting 'philosophies' – attempts to define the meanings – of causation, beauty, good, truth, the person and so forth.

Contemporary philosophy is developing an increasingly serious interest in the work of social anthropologists who write about ideas like these in non-Western societies. This is motivated more by a concern with the problems of *translation* than by the possibility of the alien concepts generating alternative philosophies. For it is only when satisfied that the former have been adequately dealt with that philosophers will allow that the latter can be reported in a different language.

Semantics is the discipline most obviously concerned with theory of language and the problems of translation, on both theoretical and practical levels. Nevertheless, the *philosopher* of language, with his critically speculative approach and *gedanken* experiments, is also in a position to develop fundamentally new theoretical perspectives on the old problems that serve to increase our understanding of what is taking place on the level of practice.

Usually anthropologists write up their expositions and analyses of the alien ideas in non-alien languages. Though they may on occasion confess to certain misgivings, the fact that anthropologists continue to produce such translations attests, if nothing else, to a continuing conviction on their part that it can be done. We are sympathetic to the explanation made by some

15

fieldworkers that they remain unimpressed by philosophers' mainly negative critiques of conceptual translation because the underlying arguments are purely abstract. In other words, philosophers appear inexcusably ignorant of the overwhelming empirical evidence – anthropological, scientific, geopolitical – that human beings from radically different cultures in the world successfully translate one another's remarks on both concrete and abstract levels and thereby communicate. We are also sympathetic to the explanation of philosophers that theirs is a second-order or abstract discipline that has no business or interest in doing fieldwork to test the theories it puts forth.

Nevertheless, in this chapter we are concerned to bring the two sides together and draw the fieldworkers' attention to the abstract arguments about translation made by a philosopher of language, W.V.O. Quine, who has for too long remained virtually unknown to them. Quine's *indeterminacy thesis of radical translation* could have revolutionary consequences for both the theory and practice of social anthropology. Since references to these consequences in Quine's own writings are rare and brief, the latter part of this chapter and the next chapter are best regarded as interpretations and applications of the thesis with some reference to the consequences for philosophy in cross-cultural circumstances and for social anthropology.

2. Underdetermination of Theory: The Relationship Between Observation Sentences and Standing Sentences

Summarizing the indeterminacy thesis in cogent yet shortened form is itself a difficult task. The most reasonably inclined slope for the attempt is Quine's general philosophy of language. In it he rejects one of Western philosophy's stronger traditions – the idea that the meanings of statements are reducible to culturally *universal propositions*. In other words the statement 'I am hungry' in English is said to have essentially the same meaning as 'J'ai faim' in French or '*Ebí ńpa mí*' in Yoruba. It is this supposedly common element of meaning that constitutes the underlying proposition, and these are the basic building blocks of any language.

Quine prefers to regard each natural language (English, Spanish, Korean, etc.) as a unique and complex theory for describing experience that conveys its own ontology, which may be distinct from that of any other. Immediate experience does not 'present' itself as ordered and categorized. It is man, with his language and the theories he uses it to construct ['The positing of bodies is already rudimentary physical science . . .' (Quine, 1975a: 67)], who defines meaning and order. 'Quine has argued at length that each of us knows what he means *himself* only relative to some background language.' (Bradley 1975: 21) And it would be linguistic ethnocentrism to presume that the meanings one culture has managed to create with its language are the same (de-tribalized as 'propositions') as those expressed or sought after by other cultures.

There is 'empirical slack' in all our beliefs ...   (Stroud 1969: 83)

When a child is learning the language of the community from his elders, he begins with what Quine calls *observation sentences* ('This is red' or 'It is raining'). Such sentences are distinctive in that, first, their truth value may vary given the circumstances (it may *not* be raining). For this reason Quine also describes them as occasion sentences. And, secondly, their truth value must be readily observable and verifiable by other witnesses who may happen to be present.

What Quine finds of particular interest in language learning is a second category of statements, described as *standing sentences*, whose truth value is relatively independent of current stimuli or occasions. This complex and important class contains all of those statements in a language that are abstracted from immediate experience and may therefore be described as *theoretical*. Theories of religion, art, politics, education and space-time, as well as notions of identity[1], rules of grammar and numbers would fall under this extremely diverse heading.[2]

A language is a kind of network or system. Observation sentences are on the periphery and linked with specific sensory experiences. Standing sentences are inside the network. They are linked to observation sentences, but may also be graded on the basis of how distant they are from experience.[3] Standing sentences are open to modification, or even falsification, but 'our natural tendency to disturb the total [language] system as little as possible would [first] lead us to focus our revisions' (Quine 1953: 44) or reevaluations upon sentences that are thought to have more specific empirical reference ('Palm trees grow on Elm Street.'), to be 'closer' to 'experience', rather than to reject any theory they would invalidate.

---

[1]'We cannot know what something is without knowing how it is marked off from other things. Identity is thus of a piece with ontology.' (1969c: 55)

[2]Quine rejects the distinction made by many philosophers between analytic and synthetic statements or knowledge. He argues that all knowledge is synthetic – has some reference to, is derived from, or is verified by experience. (See 1953. On standing sentences see 1970b: 182 and 1969c: 33).

[3]If all statements are synthetic, they can be distinguished by their '*degree* of remoteness from experience.' (Smart 1969: 5)

These statements are felt, therefore, to have a sharper empirical reference than highly theoretical statements of physics or logic or ontology. The latter statements may be thought of as relatively centrally located within the total [language] network, meaning merely that little preferential connection with any particular sense data obtrudes itself. (1953: 44)

It is when one attempts to be more specific about the *connections* between *observation* and *standing* (or theoretical) sentences that one discovers how arbitrary the latter are. Familiarity with a language on the observation level is not sufficient to predict the kinds of *theories* it will put forth on the standing level. The gap between the accidental spilling of salt and interpreting it as bad luck, between ordinary terms of reference for kith and kin and the theories of structuralism, is vast.

For this reason any number of alternative standing sentences (or theories) would fit the observation sentences of a language equally well. The standing sentences that are adopted by a particular culture are largely a matter of 'historical accident and cultural heritage'. 'The paths of language learning, which lead from observation sentences to theoretical sentences, are the only connection there is between language and theory.' (Quine 1975a:79)

Quine is therefore struck by the 'vast freedom that the form of the theory must enjoy relative even *to all possible* observation'.[4] In science, empirical evidence or observation sentences are regarded as 'the starting points and the check points of scientific theory'. Yet, because of the 'gap' or the 'empirical slack' between theory and (all possible) observations, it is likewise possible that there could be a plurality of physical theories that were 'compatible with all data and [yet] incompatible with one another'. The heliocentric theory of the solar system, when first introduced by Copernicus, was even less successful in accounting for and predicting observed phenomena than the established geocentric theory. Quine therefore concludes that 'the truth of a physical theory is *underdetermined* by observables.'[5]

What wants recognizing is that a physical theory of radically different form from ours, with nothing even recognizably similar to our quantification or objective reference, might still be empirically equivalent to ours, in the sense of predicting the same episodes of sensory bombardment on the strength of the same past episodes. (1975a: 81)

Nevertheless, Quine wants to be a 'full-blown realist' (the ontological elements of any language – e.g. trees, neutrinos, numbers, etc. – are postulated as real, as existent, subject to revision on experiential grounds) who also argues that there is a significant difference between observation

---

[4]Our italics.   [5]Our italics.

and standing sentences with regards to directness of verification and susceptibility to revision. It is this that is responsible for the greater *underdetermination* of the standing sentence.

A blood relation of the errant tradition of universal propositions is what Quine refers to as the *museum myth*. This is how he describes the persistent, unverifiable fiction that the ultimate meaning of a word is something on private exhibit in a person's 'mind'. If we, when communicating with another person, believe that we are taking our cues from, or striving to reach, that 'mind' and to understand the exhibits (meanings) it contains, then we too are victims of the myth. For in fact what we do take our cues from is their behaviour (including verbal) or overt dispositions to same.

> I do consider myself as behaviouristic as anyone in his right mind could be. (1969e (1): 268)

In other words, when I offend a friend and he punches me in the nose, I am not a party to his seething mental ego. I am a party to his red face, abusive language, and fist. And whether or not the encounter ends in my favour, my own behaviour will no doubt be affected by his disposition to respond in this manner to future abuse.

3. The Indeterminacies of Alien Behaviour

When it comes to understanding a foreign language, to translating meanings from it into our own, both errant traditions carry over. We assume that the foreigner is expressing familiar 'universal' propositions in his language. And that the terminus of communication is a foreign mental museum rather than foreign behaviour.

> Seen according to the museum myth, the words and sentences of a language have their determinate meanings. To discover the meanings of the native's words we may have to observe his behaviour, but still the meanings of the words are supposed to be determinate in the native's *mind*, his mental museum, even in cases where behavioural criteria are powerless to discover them for us . . .[6] (1969c: 28–9) This is why one thinks that one's question 'What did the native say?' has a right answer.[7] (1969e (3): 276)

It bothers Quine that a number of linguists and anthropologists give at least tacit support to these errors in their professional work, and it is partly in response to this that he develops the indeterminacy thesis of radical translation.

As in his Foreword, Quine uses the word 'native' with specific reference to indigenous language facility – as when someone is speaking their 'native' language. In this sense, anyone can be 'native'.

Note that in our text this quotation is conflated with that of the preceding footnote.

All the objective data he [the linguist] has to go on are the forces that he sees impinging on the native's surfaces and observable behaviour, vocal and otherwise of the native. Such data evince native 'meanings' only of the most objectively empirical or stimulus-linked variety. And yet the linguist apparently ends up with native 'meanings' in some quite unrestricted sense; purported translations, anyway, of all possible native sentences.

(1960: 28)

Quine's analysis of the translation exercise is with primary reference to a language that has never before been translated when a hypothetical linguist encounters it. The important points of his argument also apply to the 'established' general schemes of translation between natural languages that have been institutionalized in standardized dictionaries and language instruction. But the analysis can be more to the point and less cumbersome if modelled upon a first encounter. The issue of interest will be whether translations of standing sentences can provide real insights into and understanding of an alien culture, or whether they are intrinsically flawed by the translator's having to impose the meanings of his own language-system upon the alien one.

... radical translation: translation from a remote[8] language on behavioural evidence, unaided by prior dictionaries. (1969c: 45)

Internal to any given language, the significance of a word or statement is its meaning.[9] In *Word and Object* Quine is concerned with three levels of translated meaning(s)[10]: (a) *observation sentences*; (b) *truth functionals* or *logical connectives*; and (c) *analytical hypotheses*, the bilingual lists (or dictionary) of word or phrase meaning-equivalents that eventually serve as a systematic basis for translations of (a), (b) and, most importantly, of alien standing sentences.

With reference to observation sentences, Quine's criterion for identifying them (as a class of noises aliens make) and their meanings will, of course, be behavioural – 'dispositions to respond overtly to socially observable stimulations'. (1960: ix) For example, if our linguist observes his new-found aliens consistently making the same sound on occasions when they (publicly) direct their attention to cattle, he is justified in hypothesizing that as the appropriate translation.

Quine is careful to point out that identifying the meaning (as opposed to the noises) of an alien observation sentence is not as mechanical as the above may imply. With the frustrating 'gavagai' example, he has

---

[8]Not a cognate.

[9]Behavioural – not of the museum myth variety.

[10]'... meaning, supposedly, is what a sentence shares with its translation.' (1960: 32)

demonstrated how uncertain meaning may be on even the observational level. (How can a linguist be certain that a series of noises means 'Look at the cattle!' rather than 'Look at the undetached cow heads!'?) More than likely our linguist would be 'sensible' and, on this lowly theoretical level, presume that the alien noises amount to what someone from his own culture would say in a similar situation (e.g., 'Look at the cattle!'). But for Quine the important point is that the maxim to 'be sensible according to one's own cultural background' is *already* an imposition upon an alien language-system.[11] Alternative interpretations, alternative 'sensibles', are always possible. And an alternative interpretation might also prove perfectly satisfactory for *making* sense of all relevant alien behaviour. For there is no *one* right or wrong interpretation, no one genuine true or false. *Indeterminacy* has begun to rear its ugly head.

It is, then, possible to find examples of even observation sentences whose exact meaning would be difficult for the linguist to determine. However, because the occasions for their utterance are linked to public stimuli, observation sentences are relatively determinate in comparison with other types of statements:

> how is he [the linguist] to recognize native assent and dissent when he sees or hears them? . . . What he must do is guess from observation and then see how well his guesses work.[12]   (1960: 29)

Once he has identified the noises for assent and dissent, our linguist can further confirm alien meanings by himself voicing apparent observation sentences on apparently appropriate occasions to see if they receive an affirmative (or negative) response. Furthermore, he can propose *combinations* of established observation sentences and test, from the positive or negative alien response, whether certain alien noises which occur when sentences are combined serve as truth functionals or logical connectives (e.g. the 'not' of negation, the 'and' of conjunction, the 'or' of alternation).

> If a native is prepared to assent to some compound sentence but not to a constituent, this is a reason not to construe the construction as conjunction. If a native is prepared to assent to a constituent but not to the compound, this is a reason not to construe the construction as alternation. *We impute our orthodox logic to him or impose it on him, by translating his language to suit.* We build the logic into our manual of translation. Nor is there any cause here for apology. We have to base translations on some kind of evidence, and what better.[13]   (1970a: 82)

---

[11] As also is the assumption that such sensibility is 'common' sense.

[12] In a later commentary Quine stresses the indeterminacy underlying the linguist's powers of 'recognition' at this point. (1969e (4): 284)

[13] Quine details the indeterminacies of truth functional translation in 1969b.

Quine's reference to 'some kind of evidence' is, in effect, an admission that this process of identification is only somewhat empirical. For the linguist *begins* with the truth functionals derived from his own primary language-system. Working with alien semantic noise patterns, by a process of elimination, he tries to determine whether his language's notions of 'and', 'or', etc. 'fit'. These are then declared to be truth functionals in the alien language-system.

What if the truth functionals with which the linguist is familiar could not be paired with identifiable alien noises? Obviously the translation process would be crippled. Translating the statements of a people who appear not to honour the principle of contradiction into the statements of a people who do would be a worthless exercise.[14]

If he cannot identify truth functional equivalents, is the linguist entitled to conclude that the aliens are prelogical, illogical or that they subscribe to one of the so-called 'deviant' logics?[15] Only as a last resort – when certain that the apparent alien absurdity or silliness is not being caused by 'hidden differences of language' or 'bad translations'.

Anthropologists would undoubtedly say that this is the way they normally proceed, at least with reference to attributing illogicality to a people. What makes Quine's argument original is the use to which he puts the underlying element of indeterminacy. For the remainder of the translation exercise – the standing sentences – will prove so rife with it that these few relatively cross-cultural elements (observation sentences and truth functionals) that are open to a measure of empirical testing are to be treasured as 'shared skeletal forms' on which to drape the remainder. The translator is therefore encouraged at the outset to adopt the *convention* 'to save logical truth' at the expense of virtually everything else.

> Wanton translation can make natives sound as queer as one pleases. Better translation imposes our logic upon them, and would beg the question of prelogicality if there were a question to beg. (1960: 58).

There is a good deal more to language communication than observation sentences and truth functions. Such statements are trivial by comparison with the standing sentences of a language, which constitute its theoretical underpinnings and superstructures. As theoretical, such statements have already been characterized as non-observational. They are not linked to public stimuli that will enable our linguist to determine their meaning on the basis of dispositions to speech behaviour. In other words, *verifying* the

---

[14]So that 'It is raining' becomes 'It is raining and it is not raining', etc.
[15]For an application of deviant logic to traditional thought see Cooper 1975.

correct translation of alien noises that are said to mean 'bad luck' or 'A thing cannot be both itself and something else at the same time' is a much more imposing task than it was for 'Look at the cattle!'.

Yet linguists and anthropologists have produced countless scholarly volumes in which they record, systematize, analyse and explain in a seemingly objective manner, *as well as translate*, alien statements about their belief-systems, religious systems, world-views, value systems, etc. How can this be? According to Quine here they may be called to account.

To regularize translation the linguist begins to construct a manual of translation, a comprehensive system (dictionary, rules of grammar, numbers, etc.) for translating alien verbal behaviour into his own language. To do this:

> he abstracts native particles and constructions from observed native sentences and tries associating these variously with [for example] English particles and constructions. Insofar as the native sentences and the associated English ones seem to match up in respect of appropriate occasions of use, the linguist feels confirmed in these hypotheses of translations – what I call *analytical hypotheses*.[16]   (1969c: 33)

Given their relatively empirical character, *some* objective constraints apply to the reduction of observation sentences to (translated) component meanings in the system of analytical hypotheses. The same can be said for the meanings of truth functionals.

Nevertheless, there are likely to be a vast number of alien noises whose meanings the linguist finds it difficult or impossible to identify on the basis of observation. Among these would be the alien standing sentences. The linguist therefore shifts techniques and on a trial and error basis, supplemented by 'the sensible thing to talk about in this kind of situation would be "x"' approach, he hypothetically equates the meaning of a certain alien noise with the meaning of a certain standing sentence (theoretical element) derived from his primary language. If this provides a sensible translation of the alien noise in the context in question, and in other contexts, the linguist will likely conclude that he has found the correct meaning.

For Quine the crucial point is that the linguist cannot produce independent verification of his theoretical hypothesis. For example, let us take a term like 'destiny'. He cannot justify his claim that certain alien

---

[16]Perhaps Quine settles on the adjective 'analytical' because initially hypothetical and marginally verified equivalences are, through custom, eventually *stipulated* as *the alien meanings*.

noises *mean* 'destiny' in the same way as he did for 'cattle'. There is nothing like the grazing herd of cattle against which to test it. 'Destiny' is an abstract concept that is heavily theory-laden and interrelated with a number of other theory-laden terms, such as 'predetermination' and 'necessity'. All three of these terms are related to sensory experience and observation, but as theoretical they are also sufficiently removed from experience to make behavioural definitions impossible.

Furthermore, 'destiny' is an English-language concept. For the linguist to hypothesize that it is also an alien-language concept is *to presume that abstract meanings transcend language* – a variety of the myth of universal propositions, and ethnocentrism[17]. For him to assert that, even if not adequately verified by alien behaviour, the meaning is 'there' in the alien 'mind' is a variety of the museum myth.

The reason the linguist knows of 'destiny' as a meaning is because of *his* own natural language. There is no empirical evidence that will ever be sufficient to prove that a recurrent noise in the alien language means the same thing. The most that can be claimed therefore is, that when translated *as if* certain noises were equivalent to the English-language 'x', 'y' or 'z', alien theoretical statements: (1) make some kind of sense, and (2) do not conflict with the (relatively independently verifiable) analytical hypotheses assigned to alien observation sentences and logical connectives. Yet it is entirely possible that another linguist could come along and suggest an alternative hypothesis that also makes sense and results in significantly different translations for the relevant noises.

> There can surely be no doubt that Quine's statement about analytical hypotheses is true, though the question arises why it is important.
>
> (Chomsky 1969: 61)

As there is no independent evidence to which to appeal, there could be no crucial experiment that would prove one alternative true and the other false. Multiple systems of analytical hypotheses, equally satisfactory as explanations of alien behaviour but resulting in different translations, would mean that anything like the 'real' alien theoretical meaning would remain forever indeterminate.

> The totality of possible observations of verbal behaviour, made and unmade, is compatible with systems of analytical hypotheses of translation that are incompatible with one another. (1969e (3): 275)

---

[17] As could be his asking the aliens whether their 'destiny' is necessary or subject to change. Relating the three concepts in this way might not even be intelligible in the alien language (given that the linguist had assigned the English-language 'necessity' its own noise).

It is therefore in principle impossible to establish whether any given manual of translation is true or false. This is the indeterminacy thesis.[18]

Two supplementary points remain to be made. The first concerns the deceptively exceptional case of the bilingual, the translator who is fluent in both of the languages in question.

> The linguist who is serious . . . will steep himself in the language, disdainful of English parallels, to the point of speaking it like a native. His learning of it even from the beginning can have been as free of all thought of other languages as you please; it can have been virtually an accelerated counterpart of infantile learning. When at length he does turn his hand to translation . . . he can do so as a bilingual. (1959: 474–75).

But he cannot escape indeterminacy. Learning fluency in two different languages is one thing, translating between them is another. The bilingual errs if he translates with the presumption that the myth of universal propositions is true. He too must construct a system of analytical hypotheses.

> The differences are just that he can introspect his experiments instead of staging them, that he has his notable inside track on non-observational occasion sentences, and that he will tend to feel his analytical hypotheses as obvious analogies when he is aware of them at all. (1960: 71)

It is still the case that a second bilingual could produce translations based on meaning equivalences that were significantly different and yet of comparable explanatory weight. Nevertheless, Quine agrees that bilinguals are in the best position to cope with the problems and possibilities of indeterminacy.

Finally, can Quine be accused of trivializing the problems of translation by confusing them with those of communication generally? The indeterminacy of meanings is also a problem for those who speak the *same* language. This is something he acknowledges:

> On deeper reflection, radical translation begins at home. Must we equate our neighbour's English words with the same strings of phonemes in our own mouths? Certainly not; for sometimes we do not thus equate them. Sometimes we find it to be in the interests of communication to recognize that our

---

[18]There are obvious parallels between the arguments for underdetermination of theory and indeterminacy of translation, but it would be wrong to regard the latter as a special case of the former. Quine *is* a realist with regard to overall scientific theory, but the significance of the indeterminacy thesis is that *no theoretical alternative may be regarded as true or false*. See 1969e (3): 275.

neighbour's use of some word, such as 'cool' or 'square' or 'hopefully', differs from ours, and so we translate that word of his into a different string of phonemes in our idiolect. (1969c: 46)

In other words, indeterminacy too begins at home, though in such a situation translations are taking place between people who share one, single language culture. However, as far as Quine is concerned, the equivalent of a radical translation situation obtains when an individual is first *learning* the meanings of his own language.[19]

4. Zande Indeterminacies

Anthropologists acknowledge elements of indeterminacy in their translations. For example, in *Witchcraft, Oracles and Magic Among the Azande* Evans-Pritchard says the following:

(1) Is Zande thought so different from ours that we can only describe their speech and actions without comprehending them, or is it essentially like our own though expressed in an idiom to which we are unaccustomed? (1937: 4)

(2) My aim has been to make a number of English words stand for Zande notions and to use the same term only and always when the same notion is being discussed ... I do not want to quarrel about words, and if anyone cares to designate these notions and actions by terms other than those I have used I should raise no objection. (1937: 8–9)

(3) Along this path lie many pitfalls, because the desire to assimilate primitive notions to kindred notions of our own tempts us, in the first place, to read into their beliefs concepts peculiar to our own, and, in the second place, to interpret their beliefs by introspection or in terms of our own sentiments. (1937: 313)

Despite these expressed reservations, Evans-Pritchard feels he succeeds in translating Zande beliefs and that he is thereby entitled to evaluate the general nature (or mode) of Zande thought. This is all the more remarkable in view of the fact that he describes his own translations of Zande beliefs as 'free' rather than 'literal'. 'Readers will therefore have to take my translations on trust, but were I to give them the native texts together with literal translations they would be, all but a few, equally hopeless.' (1937: 2) The questions we must pose at this point are why Evans-Pritchard opts for free translation and what sort of meaning it can transmit.

---

[19]'For me the difference between the domestic situation and radical translation is just that domestically we can and do depend largely on homophonic translation, this being how we learned our language.' (Quine, personal correspondence, 15 April, 1980).

A free translation of language [(1) in diagram] concentrates upon giving the general sense or significance (often in summary form) of the alien verbal behaviour rather than upon correlating each alien noise with a specific (literal) meaning. Evans-Pritchard would likely claim that Zande peculiarities of syntax and meaning would make a literal translation incomprehensible. Only those could follow it who had sufficient exposure to Zande culture to interpolate the statements with reference to the appropriate context.

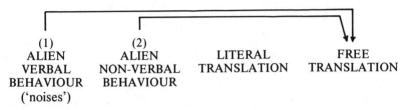

(1)	(2)		
ALIEN	ALIEN	LITERAL	FREE
VERBAL	NON-VERBAL	TRANSLATION	TRANSLATION
BEHAVIOUR	BEHAVIOUR		
('noises')			

An assessment guided by the indeterminacy thesis would find it difficult to accept this explanation. If Evans-Pritchard feels that his exposition would become virtually unintelligible if it incorporated literal translations of Zande texts, it is fair to conclude that he has not been able to work out an English-language translation manual adequate for translating Zande verbal behaviour that occurs in the company of *mangu, soroka* and *ngua*. [20] If he has not been able to work out a translation manual, then it is questionable that there is any adequate basis for the translation of the relevant Zande texts. The few who could possibly interpolate literal translations would most likely be bilinguals who can 'translate'[21] the literal English confusion back into Zande and make sense of it that way; or who would have sufficient exposure to Zande culture to do their own private *free* translations of the literal English so that the unclear statements then take on sense or significance *in English*.

Are there some special mechanics involved in the production of a free translation that enable it to succeed and convey alien meanings where a literal one has failed? Besides verbal behaviour (or speech) the only major alternative source of information available to the fieldworker is bodily behaviour, which is in fact what most people mean when they think of behaviour.[22] But it is difficult to imagine behaviour of this variety [(2) in

---

[20]The three Zande noises he translates as 'witchcraft,' 'oracles,' and 'magic'.

[21]'Associate' would perhaps be a more accurate word, since the confused English serves as a sign or mark of the original Azande rather than as a meaning equivalent.

[22]'We must now view witchcraft in a more objective manner, for it is a mode of behaviour as well as a mode of thought.' (1937: 84)

diagram] that could ever be sufficient to substitute for alien articulations of theory (much less their English-language translations).

The cumulative effect of these queries that have grown out of our discussion of free translations is to make one wonder how Evans-Pritchard is able to write as if the question, 'What does the native believe?' has a unique and correct answer. His free translations arise out of a mélange of observation, guesswork, intuition, 'the sensible thing to believe would be "x"' approach, and his own creativity[23] (this would be particularly important when there is no adequate translation manual).[24]

For example, his equivalence of the Zande '*ngua*' to 'magic' requires that relevant Zande sentences be translated so as to display the same complex natural philosophy this word is used to describe in the English language. Because 'magic' is associated with such terms as '*magician*', '*good* magic', '*bad* magic or *sorcery*', '*spells*', '*omens*', and '*evil*' in that language, Evans-Pritchard must struggle to identify Zande noises (or behaviour) that serve as their equivalents. Otherwise the introduction of the concept 'magic' would be groundless, or nonsensical.[25]

It is important to note that this discussion of free versus literal translations is not predicated on the assumption that the only satisfactory definition of an alien theoretical noise is an essentialist one, a relatively invariable core meaning that provides satisfactory translations of all statements. Quine would certainly agree that a concept may shift its meaning in different contexts. Nevertheless translation indeterminacy would also affect the identification of these shifts in meaning. Single components of any proposed cluster of meanings (or, indeed, the whole cluster) are always open to alternatives that would result in significantly different translations, and there would never be sufficient evidence to determine whether one was more true to the alien meaning than another.

Anthropologists use *modes-of-thought* words to characterize the general relations between observation sentences and standing sentences in an alien language. The English language-system has developed a number of terms – rational, emotional, mystical, common-sense, scientific, etc. – used to

---

[23]Despite his admonition: 'Above all, we have to be careful to avoid in the absence of native doctrine constructing a dogma which we would formulate were we to act as Azande do.' (1937: 82)

[24]Quine's response to our argument is: 'One effect is the repudiation of the distinction between free and literal translation.' (personal correspondence, 15 April, 1980)

[25]This might be described as the myth of universal theories. See the Index to *Witchcraft, Oracles and Magic* for references to relevant passages.

characterize such relations *internal* to it. When undertaking analyses of alien language-systems on the basis of English-language translations, anthropologists often also import these modes-of-thought terms to describe the general character of alien 'thought'.

Evans-Pritchard does so frequently in his Zande material.[26] However, from the standpoint of the indeterminacy thesis, *the only thing to which Evans-Pritchard is entitled to apply these terms is the set of English-language analytical hypotheses* he has found useful for translating the Zande noises associated with *mangu, soroka* and *ngua*. Given his difficulties with literal translations, we may query whether he has succeeded in working out a set of these hypotheses. But *if* he had, indeterminacy requires that we allow for the possibility that another translator could work out a different set of English-language hypotheses that would express different modes-of-thought. This would also serve to counter any argument that it is possible to use English-language modes-of-thought to characterize the way Azande think in their own language (rather than the way it appears in translation).[27]

5. *Introduction to an Experiment in Translation*

In a radical translation situation the alien language is similar to a secret code, and the linguist plays the role of a cryptographer who is trying to break it. He may enjoy some success in decoding alien behaviour that is used to express observation sentences and logical connectives, but the standing sentences must forever elude him.

Yet, as previously noted, anthropologists continue to produce monographs that purport to be accurate translations of alien standing sentences on every imaginable subject. The international community is heavily dependent upon standardized bilingual dictionaries that contain innumerable entries for theoretical terms. Millions of people in the world use these equivalences to communicate on an everyday basis, and do so with apparent success and

---

[26] 'Of emotional rather than cognitive significance' (xxii); 'mystical notions' (19); 'common-sense judgement' (74); 'scientific notions' (127).

[27] Evans-Pritchard's comparisons of Western and Zande practices are too vague to justify his attempts at identifying 'common' modes of thought: 'We ought rather to ask whether primitive peoples perceive any difference between the happenings which we, the observers of their culture, class as natural and the happenings which we class as mystical. Azande undoubtedly perceive a difference . . . though in the absence of a formulated doctrine of natural law they do not, and cannot express the difference as we express it. . . It is not an evident notion but transcends sensory experience. They do not profess to understand witchcraft entirely. . . They feel out of their depth in trying to describe the way in which witchcraft accomplishes its ends.' (1937: 81)

satisfaction. Surely Quine would not advocate that they all be consigned to the dustbin and that we be content with cross-cultural exchanges of the 'Look at the cattle!' variety. If he does, he would be consigned to the group of speculative critics who elicit a flicker of interest from non-philosophical circles until the practical consequences of their arguments are brought into the clear light of day.

Given the international situation, translation on the theoretical level has become a practical necessity that cannot be relinquished. But we must be clear about how much is being communicated.[28] Practical exigencies encourage cultures that come into contact to agree upon 'common' meanings. What this usually means is that, when working out a translation manual, one language must defer to the meanings of the other.

For example, if an English-Hausa/Hausa-English dictionary is compiled by an Englishman, he will work *from* English standing sentences *to* Hausa behaviour. This means that English-language theoretical entities become the paradigms for defining Hausa indeterminacies, rather than the reverse. Such a dictionary would consequently be much more useful to 'native' English-language speakers than to 'native' Hausa-language speakers.

Bilingual dictionaries that are weighted in favour of the standing sentences of one language provide only a rough and ready basis for cross-cultural communication. However, theoretical discourse is a subtle, technical and sophisticated level of expression within any language. Consequently it will suffer most in translation. This is why Quine feels that its translators must be made to realize that *their* (culturally relative) creativity and *their* (culturally relative) sense of linguistic analogy are essential rather than reprehensible elements of radical translation.

> Translation is fine and should go on . . . What 'all of this' does occasion, if grasped, is a change in prevalent attitudes toward meaning, idea, proposition. And in the main the sad fact is, conversely, that 'all of this' escapes recognition precisely because of the uncritical persistence of old notions of meaning, idea, proposition. (1969e (3): 276)

Even if the indeterminacy thesis is true, human beings will still be confronted with the very real need for inter-cultural communication. Quine recognizes this and, interestingly, after defending a radical thesis like indeterminacy so uncompromisingly, the few *positive* recommendations[29]

---

[28]'We must bear in mind that seemingly successful communication can indeed prevail where there are no empirical checkpoints to bring it up short.' (Quine, personal correspondence, 15 April, 1980)

[29]Quine rejects any attempt to treat 'Chapter II of *Word and Object* as instructions for field linguists'. (1969e (2): 271)

he makes to any 'new breed' of translators are notably conservative. It may be impossible to produce an accurate radical translation of alien beliefs. But Quine feels (apparently) that the consequences of misrepresentation and (certainly) that the degree of absurdity will be lessened if translators honour four criteria for their choices of analytical hypotheses: (1) the more *banal* manual of translation is to be preferred; (2) as is the more *simple*; (3) that manual is to be preferred which pairs what it would be *natural* to say in the same or an analogous situation in the language of translation with what is said to be said in the alien language; (4) and therefore that too which pairs what it would be *unnatural* to say in the one with the other.

> For certainly, the more *absurd* or *exotic* the beliefs imputed to a people, the more suspicious *we* are entitled to be of the translations; the myth of the prelogical people marks only the extreme. For translation theory, *banal* messages are the breath of life.[30]   (1960: 69)

The first of these criteria is that the translator favour the banal, the commonplace, the trite meaning equivalents in his primary language. This is a more precise application of the principle of language analogy[31], and would hold for translations of both observation and standing sentences. Quine's remarks therefore imply that, internal to any language of translation, it is necessary to rate observation and theoretical elements comparatively in terms of relative degrees of banality and/or exotica. The criteria that would determine such ratings are left unspecified, and this could lead to problems. Neither the banal nor the exotic can, for example, be dependably correlated with the degree of theoretical abstraction. Basic material object categories or attributes could be exotic without being very abstract.

One also wonders about the *cross*-cultural status of the banal as a criterion, given its own possible involvement with indeterminacy, as well as that of terms such as the 'exotic', the 'bizarre' and the 'absurd'. However, assessing the banal in any strict sense as such a criterion would be to misrepresent Quine. His explanation of its proper function is as follows:

> Banality is no cross-cultural criterion. It is just another way of stating the principle of charity. We put a premium on agreement of truth value, other things being equal. But there are other considerations too, and thus it is that we do come out, quite properly, with ascriptions of exotic beliefs.[32]

In other words, the translator is best advised to assume basic, shared meanings from the outset. Obviously there may also be a legitimate place

---

[30]Our italics.

[31]See p.21 above.

[32]Quine, personal correspondence, 15 April, 1980.

for exotica as well (note Quine's use of the term 'ascriptions' in the above quotation), though precisely how the 'other considerations' to which he refers would influence the translator's work in practice is not made clear.

Radical translation is, inevitably, the creation (rather than the communication) of meaning. Then why does Quine resort to the banal? Because he thereby hopes to lessen the chances of indeterminacy's being the cause (as, indeed, he believes it has been) of systems of analytical hypotheses that lead to purportedly objective but in fact silly, absurd, illogical and consequently useless as well as offensive ('primitive', 'savage', etc.) 'translations' of alien beliefs.

A second, though much less enthusiastically articulated, criterion is the *simplicity* or *neatness* of the system of analytical hypotheses that serves as a basis for radical translations of alien observation and standing sentences. Though the processes by which theoretical analytical hypotheses, in particular, are produced are so dependent upon the meanings of the translator's primary language,[33] so *ad hoc*, that the reason for preferring the simpler set of meanings is expediency rather than truth. It is easier to work with the less complicated manual of translation, provided it does not give rise to an inexcusable number of patently ridiculous translations.

The recommended model for (indeterminate) translation therefore is one in which (the most?) banal or commonplace – in effect, safe – meanings are chosen as the analytical hypotheses used to translate observation sentences. Once these have been translated, the anthropologist has no choice (assuming relevant alien discourse goes beyond the observation sentence level) but to select *theoretical* elements, also from the language of translation, that are likely to be coupled – *in* the language of translation – with the type of observation sentence in question. If certain alien observation sentences are translated into English as referring to plants that are of medicinal value, it would be silly to translate alien standing sentences relevant to their powers with concepts derived from English-language aesthetics. The theoretical elements of English-language pharmacy, or biochemistry, or herbalism itself would be more banal and therefore more promising candidates. In other words, the sense of language analogy ('We use our language to talk about "x" kind of theoretical element to explain or predict that kind of thing.') applies on the theoretical level as well.[34]

---

[33]This, after all, has been the basic problem of indeterminacy all along.

[34]It is the evidential basis for this sense of analogy that Martin Hollis and Steven Lukes dispute in their interesting published debate. See Hollis 1974; Lukes 1974; and Lukes 1973. For a more recent critical analysis of Quine's arguments that claims he provides no methodology for the translation of standing sentences see Bolton 1979.

However, in accordance with the simplicity criterion, if of two equally banal but inconsistent theoretical elements – one derived from biochemistry and the other from herbalism – the latter provides sensible translations of alien verbal behaviour in more contexts than the former, for that reason alone it is to be preferred. In fact, it is a consequence *of* indeterminacy that there can be no other reason.

The third and fourth criteria, pairing up natural with natural and unnatural with unnatural, are complementary. When he writes of the natural with reference to psychological attitudes (e.g., knowing, believing, doubting, etc.), Quine has recourse to numerous metaphors from the drama:

> In indirect quotation we *project ourselves* into what, from his remarks and other indications, we *imagine* the speaker's state of mind to have been, and then we say what, in our language, is natural and relevant for us in the state thus *feigned*.[35]　　　　　　　　　　　　　　　(1960: 219)

> An indirect quotation . . . an essentially *dramatic act*.[36]　　　(1960: 219)

> . . . the other propositional attitudes, . . . all of them can be thought of as involving something like quotation of one's own *imagined* verbal response to an *imagined* situation.[37]　　　　　　　　　　　　(1960: 219)

> *Casting* our real selves thus in unreal *roles*.[38]　　　　　　(1960: 219)

In his account of this criterion Quine clearly believes he is describing a practice translators do follow as well as recommending that they continue to do so.

> We are in effect assuming general psychological similarities also across the language barrier; and this again is good strategy. . .　　(1969e: 290)

The fieldworker who observes aliens in a variety of circumstances tends to interpret the psychological attitudes underlying their behaviour in terms of what it would be natural for him – the fieldworker – to 'feel' in an identical or analogous situation. Given the absence of other methodological options, this makes good sense. But Quine's reservations about it as an accepted practice are at least two: (1) the indeterminacy thesis always allows for significantly different yet sensible interpretations of the alien psychological attitudes; (2) what is taken as the psychological attitude 'natural' to a certain situation or certain behaviour in one culture may not be the same as in another (e.g., If I would be doubtful in that kind of situation, then they must be as well.).

One has more hope of correlation if one tries to match up, more or less, the

---

[35-38]Our italics.

degrees of bizarreness, from language to language, rather than just limiting translations to the most natural. A clue to reducing indeterminacy and making the decision [choosing between alternative translations of alien behaviour] would be to consider these degrees of unnaturalness.

(Davidson, et al., 1974: 488)

If the language of translation has some expressions for and rough way of measuring how bizarre something is, the attempt must be made to correlate this, as well, with parallels in the meaning of alien behaviour.

There is some obvious overlapping amongst Quine's four criteria, but a point for greater concern is that their combined effect, or aim, is that aliens end up behaving, or rather meaning, 'just like us'. We are encouraged to make our commonplace their own, and also our naturals and unnaturals. The Quine who rejected universal propositions (as abstract objects) as a form of ethnocentrism ('my meanings are their meanings') effectively reintroduces them (in practice) by means of the above criteria.

Somewhat paradoxically, Quine is not unaware of the possibility that aliens may in certain respects *be* very different from us. 'Incidentally we wouldn't want to be enslaved by that [the criterion of naturalness] either, because I think we want to allow the natives to find certain things natural that we don't find that natural and vice versa.' (Davidson, et al., 1974: 495) We've made reference before to the apparent problems involved in how a translator is to determine the permissible degree of alien unnaturals relative to the language of translations' naturals.

Nevertheless it *is* clear again that Quine's residual partiality for criteria like the commonplace and natural is because he feels it more important to control the chances of *indeterminacy's* being the cause (as, indeed, he believes it has been) of manuals of translation that lead to illogical and offensive 'translations' of alien behaviour. 'The linguistic ideal in any event would be a humdrum sort of discourse on the native's part and anything startling or surprising would be *prima facie* evidence of error.' (Davidson, et al., 1974: 495)

How would Quine regard the numerous published accounts of alien belief systems, based upon translations of alien verbal and non-verbal behaviour, that ignore or would reject the indeterminacy thesis? It goes without saying that the anthropologists who produce such monographs believe they are based on careful and objective criteria of translation, even if different from Quine's 'safe' and 'simple' own.

In a subdivision of Chapter II of *Word and Object* ('On the Failure to Perceive the Indeterminacy') he identifies seven of these alternative, supposedly objective techniques and criteria. However his aim is to prove that the reason translators have recourse to them is precisely because of (and thereby to camouflage, though often unwittingly) the indeterminacy underlying their work.

For example, if an alien noise occurs in a context where the meaning assigned by one analytical hypothesis cannot produce a sensible translation, the anthropologist will assign it an alternative meaning, an alternative hypothesis, for that context. Moreover he will believe that he is in fact recording a genuine variation in alien meanings. But Quine argues that it is the initial and intrinsic indeterminacy of translation in general that makes it impossible for the anthropologist to settle upon any truly determinate meaning, and therefore to have recourse to any number of *ad hoc* alternatives.

Again, if the anthropologist feels that assigning contextual meanings to the same behaviour makes his manual of translation too awkward or complex, there is another possibility. He may claim that the behaviour is false in the sense that it is misguided or misplaced. Given the meaning the anthropologist has assigned to it, a rational alien should not behave that way in the situation. Therefore the anthropologist believes he has proved that the alien is making some kind of error. Quine argues that the 'error' is likely to be surd behaviour only in relation to the anthropologist's system of analytical hypotheses. It is therefore the indeterminate meaning afforded by that system (rather than the alien meaning) that is responsible for such behaviour's being translated as patently misguided.

The indeterminacy thesis was first proposed in 1959, almost forty years ago. What have been the consequences for social anthropology? In practice, as Quine is very much aware, none. In theory, what little response there has been is understandably hostile. For if the thesis is true, the profession as it is known would cease to exist. Monographs that purport to be translations of alien beliefs become equivocal figments of intrinsically ethnocentric imaginations.

True, Quine proposes his 'safe' and 'simple' criteria as guidelines for revised, *admittedly* ethnocentric interpretations of alien beliefs. But the restrictions he imposes are so severe, the resultant level of secure communication so limited, that one wonders whether there would be any point to producing such 'translations', whether social anthropology would not fade away entirely.

At this point we should like to take into account the suggestions of two philosophers, Dorothy Emmet and Quine himself, on how to circumvent or to cope with indeterminacy in social anthropology, after they had reached this point in reading this chapter in draft form. What we find of particular interest is that, though the former would oppose the indeterminacy thesis and the latter must obviously support it, the recommendations they make appear, in one important respect, identical. First Emmet:

> What Quine's treatment brings out for me is the banality of behaviourism. It is a possible view so long as you are sticking to fairly familiar actions and observation statements; but fails to show how we can understand other speakers of the same language, let alone other languages, as soon as you get into abstractions of any subtlety. *We learn to understand each other through continual talk and shared interests, and doesn't the same go for understanding some one from another culture . . .? Isn't there hope too in the growth of a number of highly educated 'natives' who have learned to think in both thought systems . . . and who can proffer translations of terms* and phrases with abstractions in them?[39]

Then Quine:

> *Mine is not a defeatist position.* The ideal I envisage for the anthropologist is that of *projecting himself into the community to such a degree as to be able to foresee behaviour, verbal and otherwise, at least as successfully as a native might. An ideal manual of translation, then, is a mapping of sentences to sentences that would best enable this anthropologist to induct a compatriot into a similarly insightful position* vis-a-vis the behaviour of that community.[40]

If the anthropologist *can* project himself into the alien culture as successfully as the *alien* can, do any significant *practical* consequences of the indeterminacy thesis for cross-cultural studies remain? The facility and sensitivity of such an expert for cross-cultural translations could be (Quine does use the word 'ideal') of a sufficient degree to accurately convey, even if at cumbersomely greater expository length, abstract meanings between cultures.

If we are to do justice to Quine in the course of any apparent disagreement with him, two points must be reemphasized: (1) the indeterminacy thesis arises out of a *radical* translation situation – there has never been any significant communication between the two languages concerned; (2) the indeterminacy thesis is a *philosophical* thesis – it is proposed on the basis of a *thought experiment* and is not meant to be used as a practical, fieldwork guide for anthropologists or linguists. It would, therefore, be wrong to take Quine to task for having overlooked certain facts about everyday cross-cultural translations. For even though he may be aware of them, he is not concerned with them. Nevertheless this does not

---

[39]Personal correspondence, 8 April, 1980. Our italics.
[40]Personal correspondence, 15 April, 1980. Our italics.

mean that his philosophical thesis is devoid of practical consequences, and totally irrelevant to theories of translation governing situations where there is some pre-established fluency between speakers of the two different languages. Such things as the myth of universal propositions, the museum myth, and the 'gap' between the empirical and the abstract, may deserve to exercise some influence and restraint upon all processes of translation, even if at a rather deep and primordial level.

If the indeterminacy thesis in its most radical and literal form were true, there could still be some, admittedly restricted, basis on which to justify the continued production of anthropological monographs. What would then be required is a change in attitude towards the *significance* of the contents. By *hypothetically* equating certain alien verbal behaviour to certain foreign language concepts the anthropologist can *create new meanings*. He imposes the syntax and vocabulary ('Whenever this noise occurs, I will translate it as "x".') of his own language on a system of non-random behaviour that is not his language. The aliens, therefore, often end up 'saying' a series of English words that people who are English-language speakers would not say.

In other words, the loss of objectivity (from translation) is compensated for by a generous influx of creativity. The anthropologist can utilize indeterminacy to create levels of theoretical discourse in *his* own language that may be radically different from those to which 'native' speakers of the language are accustomed. 'Translations' are not what the aliens are saying in their language. They may not be what the translator would normally say in his language. They are *original* statements, *original* hypotheses that may juxtapose categories traditionally kept distinct and thereby lead to the discovery of new truth.

The controversy over the *true* meaning of the Nuer noises Evans-Pritchard translates as 'Twins are birds', or of the Nuer equivalence of 'ox' to 'cucumber', can then be seen as an example of what happens when this kind of original hypothesis (in English vocabulary and syntax) is treated as if it were what the Nuer *really* mean. The numerous incompatible interpetations[41] of these statements are efforts to make 'sense' of the same behaviour on the basis of different sets of analytical hypotheses. But if each interpetation were treated as an idea or outlook that may deserve serious

---

[41]See R. Firth, '*Twins, Birds and Vegetables*', *Man* (N.S.), 1 (1966) and correspondence in *Man* (N.S.), (1966; 1967); J. Buxton, 'Animal Identity and Human Peril: Some Mandari Images', *Man* (N.S.), 3 (1968); A. Hayley, 'Symbolic Equations: the Ox and the Cucumber', *Man* (N.S.), 3 (1968) and correspondence in *Man* (N.S.), (1968); G.B. Milner, 'Siamese Twins, Birds and the Double Helix', *Man* (N.S.), 4 (1969); Ernest Gellner, 'Concepts and

consideration *in its own right* (rather than as what the Nuer really mean), creativity, speculation and originality come to the fore.

Anthropologists would then have to be made aware of their role as theoretical innovators. If this more radical form of the indeterminacy thesis may be true, then published translations of alien belief systems become original hypotheses that deserve reconsideration and perhaps testing. Admittedly, 'originality' and 'interest' as utilized in this chapter are rather vague criteria. But as the hypotheses under consideration would span virtually the entire spectrum of knowledge – from morality and religion to medicine and physics – this is a problem that should be dealt with in terms of individual disciplines.

Many hypotheses may be so obviously false that testing would be a waste of time. Others may be so speculative that it is difficult to come up with consequences that can be tested, though for some disciplines this need not be a negative factor. But truth or intriguing speculation are fragile and rare commodities, and we should be grateful for the 'translation' that produces even a single interesting possibility.

Within the traditional framework each of the various 'schools' of social anthropology – structuralism, neo-intellectualism, Marxism, poetic-symbolism[42] – is the proponent of a different set or system of analytical hypotheses that they believe true to the meanings of alien behaviour. Within the radical framework the possibility of true meanings for standing sentences no longer exists. Incompatible methodologies and systems of analytical hypotheses would therefore now be compared on the basis of the new and interesting possibilities of meaning to which they give rise in the translator's own language.

We have no intention of defending this more radical version of the thesis, but we do feel it is worth drawing attention to it as a theoretical possibility and to the consequences for anthropology that would follow. Our own suggestion is that to assess the practical significance of the thesis we shall first have to undertake a translation experiment of our own. In the next chapter we shall attempt a concrete experiment in the cross-cultural

---

Society' in B. Wilson (ed.), *Rationality* (Oxford, Blackwell, 1970); I.C. Jarvie and J. Agassi, 'The Problem of the Rationality of Magic', also in *Rationality*; A. MacIntyre, 'Is Understanding Religion Compatible with Believing?', also in *Rationality*; and J. Buxton, *Religion and Healing in Mandari* (Oxford, 1973).

[42]Poetic-symbolism, which maintains that one cannot make 'sense' of the theoretical statements of traditional cultures in objective empirical terms, could also be regarded as a methodological rationalization by social anthropologists for their failures to develop adequate manuals of translation.

translation and expression of abstract meanings. On the basis of this experiment we shall eventually argue that, if the translator can identify the criteria governing classes of observation sentences made under the rubric of a specific alien theoretical term, a theoretical equivalent in the language of translation can be constructed that will withstand challenge and empirically prevail over other alternatives.

2. An African Epistemology: The Knowledge-Belief Distinction and Yoruba Discourse

1. Introduction

In this chapter we propose to attempt at least three things. The first is to demonstrate the dangers of assuming that such philosophically significant terms as 'know' and 'believe' in the English language have precise meaning equivalents in other, particularly African, languages. This may be another variant of Quine's myth of universal propositions but in fact, as recounted in the Introduction, we noticed that the supposed Yoruba equivalents of these terms were occurring in contexts foreign to their English-language counterparts even before we came to develop an interest in Quine.

A second is to engage in the concrete experiment referred to in the last chapter in the cross-cultural translation of select abstract meanings in an effort to determine what practical consequences, if any, follow from the indeterminacy thesis for such exercises. The third is to demonstrate and promote our own analytic approach to African philosophy by selecting for this experiment concepts that are philosophically significant in their own right – the English-language 'know' and 'believe' and their supposed equivalents in the Yoruba language. (When we say 'supposed equivalents' we are referring to those stipulated by the two existent Yoruba-English dictionaries (Abraham 1958; Oxford 1950). In the succeeding text, whenever we make reference to a translation equivalence drawn from them, following Quine we shall refer to it as from the *etm* (established translation manual).)

In what follows, making reference to several standard Western philosophical works and a bit of common-sense, we endeavour to identify to what it is that words like 'know' and 'believe' are meant to refer. We then proceed to identify their varieties, if any, their objects (what kinds of things one may 'know'), the criteria that must be satisfied before one can have a particular kind of knowledge or belief, and that are invoked when that knowledge or belief is challenged or disputed. Making use of the explanations and analyses of the *oníṣẹ̀gùn*, we then endeavour to do the same for their supposed Yoruba equivalents, *'mọ̀'* and *'gbàgbọ́'*. After comparing meanings between the two language systems with reference to these four terms we shall reintroduce Quine and, in the end, disagree with him over the degree to which indeterminacy may be a problem. We shall also argue that our analyses suggest that propositional attitudes are *not* universal.

2. Quine on the Indeterminacy of Universal Propositional Attitudes

Now of all examples of propositional attitudes, the first and foremost is *belief.* (Quine 1955: 186)

In English-language philosophy verbs like 'believe', 'know', 'doubt', 'hope' and 'want' are described as *psychological attitudes*, words meant to express a person's attitude towards a subordinate proposition. It is this latter relationship – of attitude towards statement – that has led to these same terms also being described as *propositional attitudes*. In other words, they are statements that are of the standard form, 'I believe that X' or ' I wish that X', where X is itself a proposition like, for example, 'he would register for the course'.

Psychologists, philosophers and anthropologists often presume that these propositional or psychological attitudes are so fundamentally human that they are transcultural. 'Belief, in fact, is one of the most commonplace and familiar things in the world.' (Price 1967: 24) In the English language the word may be 'believe', while in French it is *'croire'* and in Yoruba it is *'gbàgbọ́'*. But the underlying meaning, the state-of-mind each seeks to express, is the same, and further meaning equivalents can presumably be found in other language cultures.

One of the most powerful arguments against the universality of propositional attitudes arises from Quine's indeterminacy thesis of radical translation. In section ten of this chapter we shall make a more careful evaluation of the evidence for indeterminacy and also of the criteria Quine proposes for the composition of inter-linguistic translations. The primary aim of the present section is to summarize briefly his position with respect to propositional attitudes and then examine some of its consequences for cross-cultural comparisons.

With reference to indeterminacy generally, we have seen that the principal conclusions Quine wants to establish are: that it is impossible to prove there are culturally universal propositions (meanings); that verbal and non-verbal meanings, relative to any language, are learned and defined behaviourally; that the evidential gap between statements of empirical observation and statements of theoretical interpretation is more distinct and of greater significance – particularly with reference to the objectivity of *translations* of the latter – than is generally allowed.

A consequence of the indeterminacy thesis is the impossibility of ever *proving* that the meaning assigned to a word said to connote a particular propositional attitude in one language ('know') is indeed equivalent to that of a word in another language (*'mọ̀'*).

> These are the idioms of propositional attitude: 'X believes that p', 'X wishes that p', 'X expects that p', and so on. They all follow the broad pattern of indirect quotation, 'X says that p', as if to attribute to X the disposition to utter the sentence 'p' in some mood. Thus X believes that p if, approximately he will affirm p; he wishes or requests that p if, approximately, he will exclaim 'Oh that p!' or 'Alas,p!'.   (Quine 1975b: 92)

Quine argues that indirect quotations ('X says that p') share the same basic structure as statements expressing the more traditional propositional attitudes (believes that, knows that, etc.). All entail the claim that X somehow affirms a statement. What differs is the manner in which or the degree to which X is claimed to have expressed his affirmation. However, in consequence of the indeterminacy thesis, Quine would argue that the evidence available to the *translator*, including the bilingual, is never sufficient to prove that, for example, 'believe' is so accurate a translation of the Yoruba *'gbàgbọ́'* that sensible, systematic, alternative translations (including the claim that there is no Yoruba-language meaning equivalent) are ruled out. In other words, the claim that certain alien (verbal or non-verbal) behaviour is equivalent to 'believing', 'knowing', 'desiring', etc., is always relative to a *general* manual of translation whose meanings are, inevitably, indeterminate.

> Our evidence about a person's psychological attitudes will include all of his behaviour including his speech.   (Harman 1969: 19)

Indeterminacy bars the way to determinate interpretations of alien psychological attitudes. Quine nevertheless insists that certain standards or criteria must be used to distinguish good *indeterminate* translations from bad ones. However, it is first important that one illusory solution to the entire problem be ruled out. This is that it would be possible to ask the aliens[1] *in their own language*, about *their own psychological attitudes*, and thereby gain additional, sufficiently detailed information to settle upon determinate translations of them.

---

[1] We use the word 'alien' in the purely neutral sense of meaning 'belonging to something or sombody else'. So, in the context of our analysis of Yoruba concepts, English may be referred to as an alien language and vice-versa.

Quine would insist that this additional information has still to be translated and is therefore subject to the same, old indeterminacy. No matter how exhaustive the fieldworker's researches, no matter how detailed his information, a second translator could develop a significantly different interpretation of the same alien meanings.

Now let us consider the consequences of applying Quine's four criteria for good indeterminate translations to the translation of alien propositional attitudes.[2] The first criterion would require that the translator favour the banal, the conventional meaning equivalent in his primary language for translations of alien psychological attitudes. This again is an extension of the Principle of Charity, so as not to give rise to unwarranted translations that portray alien attitudes as bizarre or primitive. But with a term like 'believe' identifying the humdrum meaning, even in English, may prove problematic. In the *Oxford English Dictionary* 'believe' has three primary meanings: (1) 'accept as true or as speaking truth'; (2) 'think, suppose'; (3) 'have faith in the existence or efficacy, advisability, etc of'. How is one to go about determining which of these is the more banal?

The second criterion is the simplicity or neatness of the overall manual of translation. The justification for this is based upon expediency rather than truth. It is easier on the translator if he can work with the less complicated translation manual, provided it does not give rise to an inexcusable number of patently ridiculous translations. In accordance with this criterion, if of two equally banal (assuming there was a scale on the basis of which this could be computed) but inconsistent translations of an apparent alien psychological attitude (take, for example, the first and third definitions of 'believe' given above), one provides more sensible translations of alien behaviour in a greater number of contexts than the other, it is to be preferred.

A second alternative would be to construct a translation that allowed for translations of alien meanings using either definition of 'believe', the choice dependent upon its making sense in a given context. We have noted that Quine is aware of this alternative, and that he feels that contextual definitions may be primarily *deus ex machina*, little more than *ad hoc* attempts to disguise the indeterminacy underlying translation generally.[3]

> . . . the essentially dramatic idiom of propositional attitudes.
>
> (1960: 219)

As for the third criterion, Quine believes that most translators have always assumed that aliens were experiencing the same psychological

---

attitudes as they themselves would in an analogous situation. He repeatedly refers to the drama, to the idea of 'casting our real selves thus in unreal roles'. (1960: 219) But he does so with approval, for he can see no alternative. Nevertheless, indeterminacy always provides that another translator may improvise an alternative natural, and therefore again cautions us against *really* claiming to know that propositional attitudes are universal.

The fourth criterion requires that we do the equivalent with the unnatural. If it would be unnatural for the translator (as a member of his language culture) to express a certain propositional attitude in a certain situation, it is safer if he presumes the same holds for the aliens.

> The linguistic ideal in any event would be a humdrum sort of discourse on the native's[4] part and anything startling or surprising should be *prima facie* evidence of error.
>
> ('First General Discussion Session' Davidson, et al., 1974: 495)

Quine is aware that alien propositional attitudes may be different from our own. But he feels that an embarrassing number of translations that have given precedence to this possiblity have resulted in representations of alien attitudes that are both silly and offensive. Too much emphasis has been placed upon the bizarre and too little on the commonplace.

If there can never be sufficient evidence to support objectively true translations of alien psychological attitudes, would it not be safer to dispense with them as terms of reference altogether – at least for translation? Quine's responses to this would likely be the following. Since indeterminacy affects translation generally, agreeing to dispense with psychological attitudes would set a dangerous precedent for dispensing with the translating of all behaviour that goes beyond the simplest material object level.

Propositional attitudes, even as indeterminate, have a genuine utility as mediums of translation. Even the pretence of 'entering into' the alien's mood makes the interpretation of his behaviour seem that much more real and natural to us. Therefore let translators continue to utilize propositional attitudes as elements of language, but let them avoid defining them in 'mental' terms. An individual's mind or state thereof is by definition private. Psychological or propositional attitudes are best identified, understood and defined on the basis of patterns of overt behaviour.

It is here [the behavioural level], if anywhere, that we must give our account of

---

[4] Quine's use of the term 'native' is ironic, for the point of indeterminacy is that anyone can be an alien and thereby a 'native'.

the understanding of an expression, and our account of the equivalence that
holds between an expression and its translation or paraphrase.

(Quine 1975b: 87)

3. To 'Know' in English-Language Discourse and Philosophy

Perhaps the greatest agreement among Philosophers has concerned the
relation of knowledge and truth . . . I cannot possibly know that any sentence
is true unless that sentence is true. Hence truth is a condition of
knowledge.   (Lehrer 1974:24)

'Knowing' and 'believing' are complex and sometimes technical terms, both
in ordinary usage and that specialized area of English-language philosophy
known as epistemology or the theory of knowledge. The aim of this and the
two following sections is not to present a comprehensive or even consistent
theory of either term, or an exhaustive account of usage. Rather we shall
select judiciously, hoping to touch upon enough materials to give fair
representation of the complexity of each concept and of their interrelations
on the level of ordinary language, and at the same time laying the
foundations for interesting comparisons with what are said to be their
Yoruba counterparts.

If knowing is by definition true, then our first concern will be to determine
whether all knowing is of the same basic kind and, if not, what the varieties
are. We shall then go on to ask *why* or *how* something is or comes to be
knowledge. Or, another way of phrasing the same question, what sort(s) of
evidence must be produced, justification given, or conditions satisfied – if
the need should arise – in order to prove that what one claims to know *is*
true. This latter point will require paying some attention to the so-called
theories of truth that form one of the cornerstones of philosophical
epistemology.

Now in ordinary everyday English the verb 'to know' is generally used in a
dispositional sense; not quite invariably perhaps, but certainly the dispositional
use of it is by far the most common.   (Price 1969: 42)

There are philosophers who disagree with this and claim that 'knowing' has
a distinctive tone as a private mental state that intuitively distinguishes it
from other psychological attitudes. Therefore, when I say 'I know that p', I
am referring to that distinctive state-of-mind, or consciousness, at the
time.

Ordinary English usage, however, indicates that the word is used far
more commonly in a dispositional or behavioural sense. 'Disposition' is
here being used in the sense of latent tendency or trait. If I say that someone

45

knows his way around London, what I mean is that if and when he finds himself there, he will act in a manner that demonstrates he is throroughly familiar with that city.

Whether characteristically defined as a private and distinctive mental state, or as a latent disposition to behave in a certain manner, philosophers and ordinary usage have gone on to distinguish three different varieties of knowing: (1) knowing that (or information); (2) knowing how (or competence); and (3) knowledge by acquaintance.

'Knowing that' is certainly the most common usage, and may be implied by the other two. Bertrand Russell has sought to clarify ordinary usage by stipulating more precise criteria and renaming 'knowledge that' knowledge by description. But as we prefer ordinary usage as a base for our eventual cross-cultural comparisons, there is no need to consider Russell's theory in detail. 'Knowledge that':

> does not have the character of 'first hand encounter' which knowledge by acquaintance has. There is something indirect or second hand about it. Most frequently we get it from testimony, from reading what others have written, or hearing what they tell us. (Price: 65)

'Description' is appropriate, since this type of knowledge does involve understanding a description ('Tokyo is the capital of Japan.') that is existential in character. Nevertheless, 'when a piece of knowledge by description is analysed, it turns out to be reducible to knowledge *that*, knowledge of facts or truths' (Price: 65).

As we shall see, it is also possible to have knowledge by acquaintance of something of which one has 'knowledge that' ('I know that Tokyo is the capital of Japan. I visited the city in 1979.'). But the more interesting cases for comparative purposes, and for purposes of understanding the uniqueness of this English-language epistemological category, will be those in which something is known to us *only* by description. This includes any information we obtain from printed or oral sources, and to which we could refer in the context of the statement, 'I know X', where X is a proposition ('that Tokyo is the capital of Japan'). Hence 'knowledge that' is a clear example of a propositional attitude.

'Knowing how' to do something is used to characterize a practical skill or proficiency (such as playing a musical instrument or repairing automobiles), even when the possessor may not be said to have significant conceptual or cognitive knowledge relevant to understanding or explaining the skill. Such knowledge can also be intellectual, as in the case of the clerk who can mentally calculate the postal rates for parcels being sent through the mail.

Nevertheless, as with the majority of situations in which knowing means 'knowing how', the significance of the term attaches to a practical activity rather than, as in the case of knowing that, to a cognitive or propositional attitude directed towards something by definition true.

'*Knowledge by acquaintance*' is another variety of knowing which Bertrand Russell has sought to clarify theoretically. In ordinary usage, however, it has at least two characteristics: (1) I must know the object, event or person first-hand. 'Knowledge by acquaintance is contrasted with the second-hand or "hearsay" knowledge which we get from testimony, spoken or written' (Price: 54); (2) I must be sufficiently familiar with the thing or person so that under ordinary circumstances I will be able to recognize it again.

Because what is known is neither a fact nor a truth, acquaintance is not a propositional attitude. It is possible to have knowledge by acquaintance of a philosophical argument and still not be convinced that it is true. As for the earlier claim that 'knowing that' is entailed by the other two forms of knowing, it is difficult to imagine a situation in which one would obtain 'knowledge by acquaintance' and derive no 'knowing that'. Perhaps an encounter whose consequences were *total* confusion would be the exception. However, as one of the conditions of knowledge by acquaintance is that one would be able to recognize the thing if a further encounter should occur, total confusion would, appropriately, indicate a situation in which there is no variety of knowledge. Similarly, if I know how to do something, then I must have at least *some* information about it.

It is now time to proceed to the relationship between 'knowledge' and 'truth', the so-called *theories* of truth that have been proposed in the effort to explain *how* and *why* it is that a person has knowledge. For purposes of the representative model we are trying to construct, 'knowing that' will be taken as the primary meaning of 'knowledge', and the others as subsidiaries available for situations or comparisons wherein 'knowing that' does not seem to make sense or seems to be otherwise inappropriate. In any case, the theories of truth are mostly concerned with outlining the conditions for explaining the basis of 'knowing that'.

In the exposition and analysis of these theories of truth we shall rely upon Keith Lehrer (1974) as our basic reference. This is not because we have rated his analysis as the best of its kind, either from the standpoint of reporting ordinary usage or of developing an original theory. (His primary interest is in the latter.) But it so happens that, in the course of working out his theory of knowledge, Lehrer takes special interest in a number of issues that will prove relevant to the concerns and viewpoints of the Yoruba.

> . . . the most customary use of the word 'know'. Commonly, when men say they know they mean they know for certain, and they assume there is no chance of being in error. (Lehrer: 239)

It is because of this assumption that theories of truth are employed primarily as theories of justification or verification, steps people resort to when their 'truth' is challenged, with the eventual aim of making us agree that their truth should be our truth. The two theories we shall survey are commonly termed the Correspondence theory of truth and the Coherence theory of truth.

In the traditions of Western philosophy, the best known argument over what truths are to be taken as more reliable is that between the so-called rationalists and empiricists. The former, often typified by Descartes, argue that there are some truths that may be certified indubitable by the powers of the mind or reason alone, and then serve as a basis for all other knowledge. The latter, typified by Locke and Hume, argue that sensory experience, or sensation, serves as a basis for all the basic truths that are known, or not known, about the world. The literature reflecting the wrangling that has gone on between and within these two 'schools' of academic philosophy is vast and, for the most part, too technical to be of use in this chapter. The important point to bear in mind is that the word 'correspondence' is used for the overall theory because these basic truths, and the others derived from them, are said to correspond to and therefore accurately reflect reality.

What is of special interest in Lehrer's treatment of the correspondence theory is his account of the philosopher Thomas Reid's analysis of what the *average* man, apparently in any culture, treats as his basic truths. The average man is not so rigorously systematic in ordering them as the philosopher. Nevertheless his behaviour shows his commitment to a polyglot mixture of 'truths' that serve as the basis of an everyday and culturally distinct life.

> Some [truths], for example perceptual [truths] concerning what we see immediately before us, are in no need of justification. Though they can be erroneous . . . they nevertheless stand justified in themselves without need of independent corroboration. (Lehrer: 101)

Much of the traditional knowledge a man imbibes simply by virtue of being a member of his society shares this same character. Reid describes the justification underlying these basic truths as that of *'birth and ancient possession'*, and argues that the man who relies upon them 'in forming his plans and shaping his convictions' will be described as eminently reasonable.

> We may, in the customary affairs of life, rely upon the intrinsic guarantee of truth and the attendant justification that attaches as a birthright to various of our beliefs. They are completely justified in themselves without need of any independent information or justification. (Lehrer: 102)

It is when an argument or evidence is produced that challenges our perception or our traditions, or when an enterprise of enormous practical significance is likely to depend upon them, that the 'intrinsic guarantee of truth' is withdrawn or suspended. We have then to face the problem of what constitutes a satisfactory justification or verification of something as knowledge.

Coherence theory argues that there are no basic truths that may be directly, individually and indubitably verified. Truths do not occur in isolation from one another, but in the form of interrelated systems wherein one truth either explains or is explained by (or perhaps both) others. Any single truth that is a component of a coherent system must be consistent with the others. But as any number of alternatives might also be consistent with the overall system, the single component truth selected must 'either explain or be explained in relation to the system *better* than anything which contradicts it' (Lehrer: 164; our italics). The problems involved in defining 'better' are eloquently expressed by Lehrer:

> Little has been written on the question of what it means to say that E1 is a better explanation than E2 of F. Moreover, we shall not attempt to explicate that concept here. The hopelessness of obtaining any useful analysis militates against the attempt. (Lehrer: 165)

However, the major problem with the coherence theory is that it is in practice possible to develop *a plurality of systems*, all purportedly true, 'that are equally satisfactory from the standpoint of explanation' (Lehrer: 181). The dilemma, then, as Lehrer puts it, is that:

> We are left with the problem of *inconsistent* systems of [truths] having a maximum of explanatory coherence. (Lehrer: 181–82; our italics).

There have been any number of attempts by philosophers to formulate a supplementary criterion that would provide for choosing one from amongst this plurality of coherent systems. One of the more popular has been *simplicity*, but it has been found difficult to define it clearly, and to decide precisely what elements (postulates, basic concepts, ontology, etc.) of a system it is most important *be* simple. In consequence Lehrer concludes that neither simplicity nor any other criterion has yet to be produced that is an adequate or reliable guide.

We have chosen 'knowing that' as our paradigm of ordinary usage in the

English language. Does ordinary usage express any preference with reference to a theory of truth? What we should like to do at this point is to review the position of Thomas Reid, that of the so-called 'average' man and his truth(s) of birth and ancient possession.

Reid does presume that the average man operates on the basis of a form of correspondence theory. Perceptions correspond to what actually exists or is taking place in the world, and traditions (shall we call them 'social truths'?) are worth learning and applying because they are based upon factual knowledge.

Unlike the philosopher, the average man is not concerned to rigorously systematize nor to prove in advance everything that he is prepared to assert as true. It is only when his truths are challenged by others that he will concern himself with justification. And as he operates on the basis of correspondence, his initial justification should consist of proving that his *account of* his perceptions or that his *knowledge of* his traditions is accurate. If either of these is not accepted by the challengers, and the justification must proceed to a deeper level – that of proving the truth *of* the perception itself or the truth *of* the tradition itself – then obviously further proofs of correspondence will come into play.

Coherence theory – that there are no basic truths – seems less likely to be taken up by the average man and more the domain of the academic philosopher. Correspondence theory can identify and correct inconsistencies in a set of truths as effectively as coherence theory, and such notions as 'explanatory coherence' and 'simplicity' are of so technical a nature that it is difficult to translate them into average or ordinary terms. Therefore, from this point onwards, we shall incorporate correspondence theory into our model of 'knowledge' in the English language.

4. To 'Believe' in English-Language Discourse and Philosophy

Belief, in fact, is one of the most commonplace and familiar things in the world. (Price: 24)

The above quotation may give the impression that the definition and analysis of 'believing' will be easier than that of 'knowing'. In fact the opposite will prove to be the case. Arriving at a non-controversial definition of 'believe', either from the standpoint of ordinary usage or epistemological theory, is a difficult task.

Price (1969) and Needham (1972) will serve as our primary sources. They themselves disagree in their conclusions about the meaning of 'belief' in the English language. This is interesting because the two published their conclusions contemporaneously yet independently of one another. Price's analysis antedates Needham's, but the latter admits to being unaware of it until his own was virtually complete.

As with 'knowing', we will divide up our analysis between the varieties of belief and the criteria (in respect of justification or verification) of belief. This will first be done from Price's point of view and then, again, following Needham.

With reference to the varieties of 'believing', the first problem that must be dealt with, as in the case of 'knowing', is what is the best method for analysing the meaning of 'belief' generally. English-language culture has to date devised two major, alternative methods that claim to be able to do this.

The oldest is that belief is a unique kind of mental occurrence or act that can be introspected by the person who experiences it. Price describes this theory as traditional Occurrence Analysis. Its primary aim is to provide a careful, introspective analysis of the mental 'tone', characteristics or qualities of this distinctive state of mind.

The second, Dispositional Analysis, rejects the idea that belief is a distinctive state of mind. We may find ourselves affirming that we believe something, but it is wrong to regard this as a state of *mind* that can be uniquely characterized. Believing is behaving, and if we attribute it to ourselves or to another person, what we mean is a conditional statement (If p, then q.) to the effect that the person referred to would say, do or feel a certain something if a certain kind of situation were to arise.

Over and above the question of whether belief in general is best understood as a mental act or disposition, English-language philosophers have catalogued at least three different senses in which the term is used in ordinary discourse: (1) 'believing that'; (2) 'believing a person'; and (3) 'believing in'.

Believing 'that' is by far the most common usage. It occurs when the verb 'believe' is followed by the relative pronoun 'that' and it, in turn, by a proposition (as in 'I believe that it will rain tomorrow.') The object of belief, the proposition, may be either true or false – it may or may not rain. Obviously, this sense of 'believe' expresses a propositional attitude.

Less frequently we speak of believing a person, as in the proverbial case of the man who complains; 'She told me we would get married and *I believed her.*' Price argues that there is a logical connection between believing a person and believing 'that'. For we come to believe (or not to believe) a person on the basis of our experience of his previous true (or false) assertions.

The English language allows one to believe 'that' (a proposition is true or false) or to believe a person to varying degrees:

> You may believe . . . very firmly, or fairly firmly, or mildly. A rough scale of degrees of belief may be constructed, ranging from conviction at the top end to suspecting at the bottom end, with varying degrees of opinion somewhere in the middle. (Price: 39)

However, those who choose to use the word 'believe' in the third sense, believing 'in', reject the idea of varying degrees, and usage allows them to do so. They insist that one must be *absolutely* convinced of what one believes (as in the context of religious commitment). Anything less may be designated 'opinion', 'being almost certain', etc. but not 'belief'.

> . . . in the special case of believing, the two questions 'what is your evidence for . . .' and 'what are your reasons for . . .' amount to pretty much the same thing. (Price: 93)

When it comes to the *justification* (reasons) or *verification* (evidence) of beliefs, and the consequent appeal to something more than other beliefs to provide this, English-language epistemologists have identified four basic sources of evidence: perception, self-consciousness, memory and testimony. The arguments and literature relating to the first three of these are again vast and it would be a hopeless task to try and summarize them here. We shall therefore wait until the Yoruba material has been introduced, and then work backwards – *from* it *to* relevant English-language comparisons and contrasts.

The fourth source of evidence, testimony, does deserve immediate attention. This is because it is comparatively underrated by English-language philosophers, and because it would seem especially relevant to evidence for beliefs in a culture like that of the Yoruba, which is often said to be based upon oral tradition. 'Testimony' refers to information which I receive from someone else and of which, consequently, I do not have first-hand experience.

> The whole point of testimony is that it is a substitute for first-hand experience, or an extension of first-hand experience, whereby each of us can make use of the experiences which other persons have had. (Price: 117)

Price cannot envisage a society that would function or survive if it rejected testimony as a source of belief. The percentage of our beliefs that are derived from direct, first-hand experience is tiny by comparison with the percentage derived from testimony. If we insisted upon attempting to verify everything for ourselves, all forms of social cooperation would cease. Price therefore posits a *Principle of Charity* as an attitude that he feels does underlie our behaviour and therefore serves to illumine it: 'Accept what you are told unless or until you have specific reasons for doubting it' (127). He also argues that there is a moral dimension to the principle (and belief itself) in that part of its meaning is 'every person, just because he is a person, has at least a *prima facie* claim to be believed' (114).

Several ancillary consequences follow from this analysis of testimony that may prove important to us later on:

(1) 'Belief' is an area where the theory of knowledge and moral philosophy overlap.

(2) If a belief held on the basis of second-hand testimony is subsequently verified by first-hand experience, the testimony becomes redundant.

Finally, Price finds himself grown weary of the endless appeals to *public verifiability* as the ultimate test of the rationality of testimony or belief. There is no corporate 'public'. Nor is there a corporate 'Science' to perform these tests. Both are composed of individuals, and in the end – even as scientists – people will still be accepting or rejecting one another's testimony as a basis for their beliefs. It is more representative to focus attention on the problems common to accepting testimony in any forum. There *is* always a risk involved. But the (English-language) Principle of Charity admonishes that:

> it is reasonable to take this risk, and unreasonable not to take it. If we refuse to take it, we have no prospect of getting answers, not even the most tentative ones, for many of the questions which interest us.   (Price: 128)

In *Belief, Language, and Experience* Rodney Needham complains that many Western ethnographers treat the philosophy of mind they inherit from their own language systems as a kind of received truth whose categories are honoured universally.[5] Their concern, therefore, is to locate the equivalents in non-Western languages for terms such as 'knowing', 'believing', 'doubting', 'willing', 'hoping', 'desiring', 'intending', rather than in considering whether the propositional attitudes of an alien language express an entirely different philosophy of mind. Consequently, with special reference to belief, English-language anthropological monographs make constant reference to 'beliefs', 'belief systems', 'ritual beliefs', 'religious beliefs', 'primitive beliefs', and so forth.

Needham proposes that a necessary step towards determining whether 'belief' can be of value to cross-cultural studies is to be clear about its meaning in the English language. That the language has produced and

---

[5] A thesis with which Quine would obviously agree. Needham, however, makes no reference to him in this book.

preserved the words belief/believe would seem to imply that they denote something distinctive. Whether belief be regarded as a mental act, a behavioural disposition, or an epistemological category, what are the empirical grounds in support of any or all of these?

The argument that belief is a distinctive form of mental state or experience is found to be empirically unacceptable. Inner states are private and non-empirical. As for the (public) dispositions or non-verbal, behavioural manifestations of belief, in English-language culture there do not seem to be any. The only remaining behavioural possibility is 'people's *statements* about their *apprehensions, intuitions, awareness and other subtle modes of experience*' (Needham: 15; our italics). In standard analytic fashion the latter three are reduced to the first when Needham concludes, again because feelings are private: 'Is there a feeling . . . of belief itself? The issue can be publicly resolved only by resort to *the facts of language*' (Needham: 94; our italics). Statements, as public pronouncements, are empirical in their own right. Therefore what is it people *say* about belief.

If one attempts to collate the various usages, it becomes apparent that 'the general notion represented by the English verbal concept of belief is complex, highly ambiguous, and unstable' (Needham: 43). To 'believe' can mean to trust, to assess something as true, or to have faith (though what this means, even in a Christian context, Needham finds confusing).

Philosophers and religious thinkers who have tried to clarify the meaning of 'believe' have, again, proposed such diverse alternative analyses that:

> the overriding conclusion is that more than two hundred years of masterly philosophical application have provided no clear and substantial understanding of the notion of belief. (Needham: 61)

Because of its ambiguity and vagueness, 'belief' does not merit classification as a concept. This is why Needham refers to it as a notion.

Needham turns to the methodology of Wittgenstein to identify the species of minotaur he has unearthed and to lead him out of the labyrinth of meanings. Inspired by the former, he reissues the warning that 'a word does not entail the existence of a thing that corresponds to it' (Needham: 128). He then restates his earlier conclusion that clearly there is no single, essential definition of either 'belief' or 'to believe'. Furthermore, when one analyses the various usages, they do not evidence sufficient shared properties for them even to be characterized as united by Wittgenstein's family resemblances.

> I must stress that this confusing situation is not merely a result of the fact, to which we have repeatedly adverted, that a classificatory concept –

particularly perhaps a psychological one – is characteristically composed of numerous connotations bearing family likenesses one to another. It is not just that it is difficult to isolate one distinct or definitive meaning from the concept of 'belief', and then to match it to an equally discriminable meaning isolated from an alien verbal concept that is thought to be somewhat equivalent to the English word. The fundamental source of obscurity and misunderstanding is that the grammar of 'belief' does not permit anything like the precision of analysis and exactitude of expression that ideally we require in the determination of human capacities.

(Needham: 233)

'Belief' is therefore best described as an 'odd job word' (Needham: 124). It has been pressed into service by English-language culture for diverse reasons and picked up diverse meanings 'suited' to diverse contexts. 'Belief is an artifical contrivance for the convenience and advantage of society' (Needham: 150). It is a convention, a tradition, a socially acceptable noise that evokes inconsistent and ambivalent contextual meanings. But it is not a concept with genuine empirical content. 'The grammar of belief tells us that there is no such object.' (Needham: 131)

If this is the conclusion Needham comes to about the varieties of belief, he can have nothing of a more positive nature to say about the criteria for verification of this non-empirical notion. The consequences of his arguments for cross-cultural translation also are serious. If it is not possible to find a definition of the term in English, it would be odd to claim that it has an equivalent in an alien language. He is willing to concede that some bodily signs may be universal to mankind and 'can be mutually recognized independently of their social and linguistic forms'.[6] But as belief is not in this category, and as it is an English-language convention, it is best that attempts to impose it upon (or transplant it into) alien systems cease altogether. They only serve to obscure the possiblity that such systems may offer different epistemological categories and viewpoints that have as good *prima facie* objective grounds as those made familiar to us by our primary language.

The differences between Price's and Needham's positions are irreconcilable. The former argues that belief has different but determinate usages and that it is a cultural universal. The latter argues that it does not have determinate usages and therefore there is no basis for extending its use beyond the English language. We shall somehow have to choose between the two.

Needham's approach is certainly unique. He writes as a social

---

[6] A point developed by Vernon Reynolds in a paper entitled 'Man also Behaves', in *The Limits of Human Nature* (ed. J. Benthall), Allen Lane, 1973, pp. 141–157.

anthropologist, working upon the language of his own culture, using a methodology borrowed from analytic philosophy. It is his anthropological approach, we presume, that causes him to lump ordinary usage and philosophical theories, as both products of the same English-language culture, together.

This is something philosophers would resist, and it is important to understand why. If we make use of the first-order, second-order distinction, ordinary usage (the way people who speak the language in everyday life use the word 'believe') is a first-order enterprise. It is commonplace to find that such usages are inconsistent with one another and that the criteria distinguishing them are not always clear, or even articulated. The philosopher who takes an interest in the confusions of everyday language may therefore choose to go a step further and recommend a (second-order) *theory of* belief, which would have serious practical consequences that involve clarifications and changes in ordinary usage.

The important point is that such a theory of belief is not meant simply to *reflect* ordinary usage. It is meant to *reform* it. Consequently it will almost certainly be inconsistent with ordinary usage on a number of important points. When Needham lumps these first and second-order approaches together, as products of the same language culture, these inconsistencies become more and unfairly exaggerated.

Price does honour the first-order, second-order distinction in his analyses and is thereby able to maintain order over the various levels of meaning 'belief' has taken on in English-language culture. For this reason we shall prefer his model when it comes to making comparisons between this term and possible Yoruba-language equivalents.

We do, however, appreciate the attention Needham draws to the importance of looking at a language and its philosophies as a cultural vehicle or viewpoint. English-language philosophy, and concepts, are too often taken as paradigms. Even Price is guilty of this, as evidenced by the quotation that introduces this section (see above). We shall therefore endeavour, at some point, to speculate about the cultural, as well as theoretical, significance of the differences between the epistemological systems that arise from 'knowing' – 'believing', '*mọ̀*' – '*gbàgbọ́*'.

5. *Relations and Comparisons Between 'Knowledge' and 'Belief'*

Belief is often contrasted with knowledge . . . Knowledge is what we aim at in all our enquiries and investigations. But often we cannot get it. Belief is a second best.   (Price: 72)

Our aim in this chapter is to do more than tabulate the various kinds of knowing and believing. We hope to arrive at representative theories of knowledge and belief, derived primarily from common usage. One point of these theories will be to specify the conditions or criteria that must be satisfied in order for a person to know or to believe something.

We have selected 'knowing that' as our paradigm of 'knowledge', and the correspondence theory of truth as the basis upon which the criteria for its verification or justification should be interpreted. Our choice was influenced by considerations that the former is the most common usage and is entailed by other usages, while the latter best represents the theoretical viewpoint of the 'average' English-speaking person. We have yet to make similar headway with 'belief'. We may prefer Price's methodological approach to Needham's, but we have still to determine whether any one of Price's meanings is primary, and the importance of testimony (and evidence generally) to it specifically.

Agreeing upon a primary meaning for comparative purposes is a fairly straightforward task. 'Most commonly, the verb "to believe" is followed by a that-clause' (Price: 38). That this is also the meaning suitable for a comparison with 'knowing that' is demonstrated by Price's arguments that there is no common basis on which to contrast the meanings of 'knowing' and 'believing a person', of 'knowing how' and 'believing', or of 'knowing' and 'believing in'. In other words, by a process of elimination, the only contrast remaining *is* between 'knowing that' and 'believing that' (as long as we bear in mind that 'knowing that' is itself contrasted with 'knowledge by acquaintance' as *its* second-best). Our English-language hierarchy, then, is actually three-tiered:

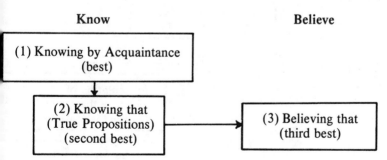

According to English usage, if a person 'knows that' X, then X must be true. The same does not hold with believing. What a person believes may be false. In fact every person in the world could believe X and it could be false.

Nevertheless, people do refer to a belief as 'reasonable' because there is at least a certain amount of evidence in support of it. And the ordinary presumption is that a reasonable belief more or less corresponds to whatever it is meant to represent.

A correspondence model for the verification or justification of knowing and believing may, therefore, be constructed along the following lines:

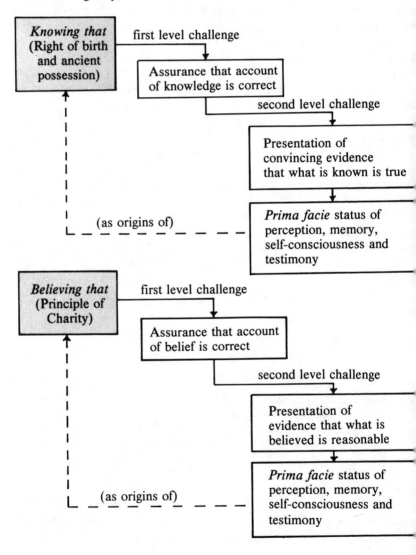

In each case the challenges to what is known or believed are two-tiered. The challenger is first concerned to determine whether the person has said what he in fact knows or believes. Once this has been established, if the challenger is still not satisfied, he will go on to challenge the knowledge or belief itself. The onus will then be on the person to present evidence that his knowledge is true, or that his belief is reasonable.

When Lehrer introduced Reid's *right of birth and ancient possession*, he made reference to an 'intrinsic guarantee of truth' that attaches to certain areas of experience. His favourite example was perception:

> In general, men think there is very little chance that such beliefs[7] are erroneous. If I believe I see something . . . then I shall believe there is so little chance I am in error that I readily repudiate any competing hypothesis and claim complete justification for my belief.
>
> (Lehrer: 188)

Lehrer's rhetoric strongly implies that he is speaking on a culturally universal level, and this we would in principle question. Nevertheless even in culturally relative terms his point, expanded a bit for purposes of our special evidential interests, would be that in English-language culture information derived from perception, memory, self-consciousness and testimony is *prima facie* true.

The evidence a person has for a proposition is what justifies him in taking either a knowing or believing attitude towards it. But with reference to testimony, in particular, it is not clear how its role differs when comparing 'believing that' with 'knowing that'.

> . . . each of us depends on testimony for almost all that he claims to *know* about anything which is beyond the range of his own first-hand observation and memory. (Price: 113; our italics)

> According to our ordinary way of thinking, testimony is one of our most important sources of *knowledge*. (Price: 112; our italics)

What percentage of 'knowing that' is on the basis of first-hand observation? Most of the factual information people claim to 'know' from reading books, for example, is second-hand. That such information is in fact true is not, and often could not be, confirmed by the readers' first-hand experience. Yet, given ordinary usage, it is more often than not classified as 'knowing that'.

It may well be that much of the knowledge by description which we ordinarily

---

[7]Lehrer's use of 'belief' rather than 'knowledge' in this passage is a consequence of his revisionist theory of knowledge, in which what ordinary usage terms the latter he terms the former (Lehrer: 239).

claim to have is belief rather than knowledge, if only because so much of it depends on testimony, spoken or written, and the reliability of the testimony is often taken for granted without much or any investigation.

(Price: 73)

The physical and social sciences (including history) devote much of their time and energy to elaborating methodologies which may be used to verify or to justify 'knowing that' claims. But that is not the point at issue. What we are interested in trying to understand is why, in ordinary usage, many propositions that do not in fact fulfil the conditions of knowledge are normally referred to as if they do. With reference to 'believing that', Price has exonerated this practice by hypothesizing a Principle of Charity. But if Charity were extended to 'knowing that', the distinction between the two would collapse. Truth, not Charity, is a condition of knowing that.

The *right of birth and ancient possession* does provide *prima facie* support for knowledge based upon perception, etc. In this respect its role (with reference to knowledge) is analogous to the Principle of Charity (with reference to belief). But this analogy is only of passing interest, for it still offers no solution to the stubborn problem of how to determine, once correspondence is challenged, at what point sufficient evidence has been introduced to support a knowledge claim. The confusion in the English language about the epistemological status of testimony reinforces this point and perhaps even justifies regarding the problem as a dilemma.

6. *The* Oníṣẹ̀gùn *Explain* 'Mọ̀' *in Yoruba-Language Discourse and Thought*

(1) The one you use your own eyes to see and which your ọkọ̀n witnesses you that it is òótọ́ – this is the best.

(2) It is clear in my eyes. This means that I have witnessed it myself. It is òótọ́ that he does this thing . . . It is clear in your eyes.

In these two quotations the *oníṣẹ̀gùn* state the conditions that must be satisfied for something to be regarded as *imọ̀*.[8] There appear to be two. The first is that the experience *must* be first-hand. The person who claims to *mọ̀* must literally have seen the thing himself. 'You see (*rí*) it before you *mọ̀* it.'

The verb '*rí*' refers to visual perception ('This one is clear in my eyes (*ojú*).'), and it is considered clearer and more reliable than other forms of sensation:

---

[8]The noun form of '*mọ̀*'.

(3) The one you see is better.

(4) If you see something, the first time it smells, the second time it smells, and when you come across the smell the third time you will *mọ̀* it. If it smells only once [and you do not see it], you will not *mọ̀* it. You will simply say that *some*thing around is smelling.

(5) If you *mọ̀* it [by touch], you have already *mọ̀* [by sight] what you put there. If I close my eyes now, and I touch (*fi ọwọ́ kan*) this funnel, I will *mọ̀* that it is a funnel. Or this cup. If I touch the cup and I *mọ̀* it, it is because I have *mọ̀* [by sight] it before.

(6) If you had not seen it before, and you touch it, you touch it in vain. Because the person you *mọ̀* from before – if you do not see him but you touch him – you cannot *mọ̀* him.

We conclude that perception has a *prima facie* status, in that it alone of all the senses is a necessary condition for *ìmọ̀*.

We must now turn to the correlative element of cognition – the witnessing of the *ọkọ̀n* (*ẹ̀rí ọkọ̀n*). This is the second condition that must be fulfilled in order to have *ìmọ̀*.

(7) You *mọ̀* this is a cupboard. If another person told you it was not a cupboard, you would insist it was a cupboard and that you *mọ̀* it very well. The witness of your *ọkọ̀n* (*ẹ̀rí ọkọ̀n*) would support you in saying that it is a cupboard. This white bottle – if they say it is black, you would *mọ̀* very well that it is white. It is clear in your eyes that it is white. I *mọ̀* that it is white.

Ọkọ̀n is the Yoruba word for both 'heart' and 'mind' or 'apprehension'. Although the former is identified as the physical correlate of the latter, the Yoruba often intend to give preference to one of the two meanings in discourse. In the above quotations the intended meaning is 'mind' or 'apprehension'.

Ẹ̀rí ọkọ̀n – your mind witnessing something *'for'* or *'to' you* – indicates *self*-consciousness. But it also indicates *comprehension* and *judgement*. As well as seeing the thing first-hand, one must also comprehend what one is seeing and judge that one has done so:

(8) It means that your *ọkọ̀n* does not witness the thing –whether it is or is not. This is when you see something, but you are having two thoughts about it.

(9) You can be invited to go and visit a person. You could say, 'If you are going to so-and-so's house, I'm not going'. Your *ẹ̀rí ọkọ̀n*[9] tells you not to go.

---

[9]The meaning of this expression in certain areas of Yorubaland has been altered by the Christian habit of making it the equivalent of the English-language 'conscience'. We feel that restricting it to a moral sense is not representative, and that the original meaning is rendered more accurately by 'judgement'.

And if you are dragged there, and it happened there is a quarrel, you will say that you did not want to come, that your *èrí okòn* told you not to come there. It is your *èrí okòn* which tells you whether something is good (*dára*) or bad (*burú*), and this is more important than accepting advice from someone. If your *èrí okòn* speaks with you, it will be difficult for another person to persuade you from doing what you want to do.

(10) This is what warns one. If I like you, my *èrí okòn* will tell me if you are not there [it will be responsible for my noting your absence]. But if I don't like you, and I want to do harm to you, and I see you and greet you cheerfully, yet my *èrí okòn* will tell me that I don't like you.

Anything that I *mò* is *òótó*. If the first quotation in this section of the paper (*rí + èrí okòn* ⊃ *òótó*) is compared with the first quotation below (*òótó* ⊃ *rí + èrí okòn*), it appears that the relationship between these two terms is a symmetrical one. The established manuals of translation (etm) translate *òótó* as 'truth'. This we may provisionally accept, as long as we bear in mind that it is 'truth' as defined by the conditions stipulated by the above relationship:

(11) It *is* [emphasized] *òótó* that this motor vehicle stands here. If people say that the motor vehicle does not stand here, you will say that you use your own eyes to see it – that it is *òótó*. You should not have two thoughts.

Òótó appears to be a property of certain forms of experience *and* of statements recounting that experience:

(12) If we are talking about something, some of it may mean nothing, and some may mean truth. Concerning speech: some have the gift of speaking, some people are known for telling lies, while some will be telling the truth. If you are speaking you may be telling lies or you may also be telling the truth.

When *imò* is challenged, an argument (*àríyàn jiyàn*) results. *Verification* is obtained by empirical testing (*o séése/kò séése*);

(13) If you see (*rí*) something and you say we should do it, I may say, 'Let us try it' – to see if it will be *séése* (possible). If it is not *séése*, we will say, '*Kò séése*'. But that which we say is *séése* is what we lay our hands on [try] and that is [proves to be] *séése*.

Justification is obtained by explanation (*àlàyé*):

(14) They can explain (*làyé*) to each other. One [of the disputants] can say, 'This thing you say you *mò* – who has ever done this in your eyes before?' The other may reply that, 'On that day I was there with somebody X [expression for name of anyone]'.

(15) The way they can take [to settle an argument] is that [asking of one disputant], 'What do you see (*rí*) that you say this?' He will explain (*làyé*) it. [Then asking of the second disputant:] What you, the other person saw before [so that] you refused to agree with that person.

An African Epistemology

The fundamental problem with regards to arguments over *imọ̀* is that one disputant has not seen first-hand what the other claims to have seen. If it is possible for the disputants to empirically test one another's *imọ̀* (as above), and thereby see for themselves whether they are *òótọ́*, the argument may be resolved. But the Yoruba are well aware that such direct testing may not always be possible. In this case, the argument must be resolved by a more circuitous route. For, if testing is *not* possible, there is no way that the *imọ̀* of one man can become the *imọ̀* of another.

The first step is to encourage each of the disputants to state fully the *imọ̀* to which he lays claim. Then, if the dispute is to be resolved, one of two things may happen. First, there may be another *witness* (the 'third person') to one of the contesting *imọ̀*:

(16) I may say, 'I hear the sound of the rain'. Someone [else] will say, 'It is not true (*òótọ́*) that you hear it' [e.g., there is a sound, but he disagrees about it being the rain]. If a third person says that he does not hear it, but hears the sound of a motor vehicle, you see now that the third person has cleared the matter.

Here the three are in the same place at the same time. But it may also happen that the 'third person was a witness to only one of the contesting *imọ̀* (to complete the passage in quotation 14):

(17) And if that third person witnessed it [thereby verifying one of the contesting *imọ̀*], the other man who is making the argument would say, '*Mo gbàgbọ́*.'

We shall come to the meaning of '*mo gbàgbọ́*' shortly, but the 'third person' is an interesting phenomenon in its own right. Given the regularity with which it occurs in the explanations of the *oníṣẹ̀gùn*, it assumes the status of an epistemological idiom that may be compared, in a very rough and tentative manner, with the Ideal Observer (Brandt 1959) in contemporary moral philosophy:

(18) [If there is a dispute (*àríyànjiyàn*) between two people:] the first were to say, he saw (*rí*) you dancing, but the second said you were not the one dancing.

We can say he forgets. We would assume that he does not put his eye on things properly.

Suppose the person said that *was* what he saw.

They could invite a third person to confirm [it], and who will tell him that he does not put his eye on things.

Is it possible for the two of them to agree that you were the person dancing?

Yes. This would mean that their *èmí*[10] work together.
Is it not possible that the *two* of them could say that you are *not* the person dancing?
It is not possible.

The 'third person' fulfils the epistemological ideal of what a perfect observer would *mọ̀*, if he existed. The 'third person' cannot pretend ignorance and his agreement, once given, cannot be withdrawn. But this raises a problem, again analogous to that faced by the Ideal Observer theory. Does the 'third person' agree because it is *òótọ́*, or is the *òótọ́* that with which the 'third person' agrees?

We said above that if testing is not possible, one man's *ìmọ̀* cannot become another's (because he is not able to see it for himself). This means that if the 'third person' corroborates one of the disputants, the other – even if persuaded – cannot then also claim to *mọ̀*. The most he can claim is that now he can *gbà* with the others, or *gbọ́* the others. It is therefore now appropriate that we deal with the conflation of these two terms – *gbàgbọ́*.

7. The Oníṣègùn *Explain* 'Gbàgbọ́' *in Yoruba Language Discourse and Thought*

(19) You can ask whether I *gbà* that you should come tomorrow, that you should come or not come. I may reply '*Mo gbà*'. This means 'I approve'.

(20) If a person did something and when they asked from me, I will say, 'I've already heard (*gbọ́*) [it]'. It means that he has told me.

The established manuals of translation make '*gbà*' equivalent to 'agree', 'accept', and 'receive'. '*Gbọ́*' is translated as 'hear', though as the ensuing quotations will indicate, it is a 'hearing' whose meaning encompasses understanding or comprehension of what is being said as well as auditory sensation. Their conjunct, *gbàgbọ́*, which is our primary interest, would therefore literally translate as 'agreeing with what one hears' or 'receiving what one hears'. We prefer the slightly more figurative rendering of 'agreeing to accept what one hears from someone':

(21) What you use your own eyes to see – this is not what you are told. What you are told may not be true (*òótọ́*). But if you use your own eyes to touch it, like this [gesture], you will understand (*yé*) it. You've used your own eyes to see it.

---

[10]A term whose meaning can shift significantly between contexts, but here probably being used in the sense of '*inú*' – the locus and source of serious or 'deep' thought.

(22) If you have been noticing the behaviour (*iwà*) of a person, we can say, 'He can do a certain kind of thing'. But if he has not done such a thing in [before] your eyes, you will say, '*Igbàgbọ́*'. But if he has done such a thing in your eyes, you will say, 'I *mọ̀*'. This means it is clear in your eyes.

(23) It means that your *ọkọ̀n* does not witness the thing – whether it is or is not.

'*Gbàgbọ́*' is considerably more difficult to analyse and translate than *mọ̀*, for it is used to characterize information gathered from and in a wider and more complex variety of circumstances. Nevertheless we may begin by saying that its negative conditions, as indicated by the above, are that one does not see the thing for oneself, and that consequently there is no opportunity for the *ọkọ̀n* to witness it. Its positive condition we shall for the moment leave simply as 'what you are told', what is second-hand.

Though the *oníṣẹ̀gùn* do not explicitly identify different varieties of *igbàgbọ́*,[11] we find it helpful (for purposes of analysis) and, we believe, also representative to distinguish four. If one reduces this verb to its two separate components, the application of negation produces four logical possibilities: (1) Hearing and Agreeing (p . q); (2) Hearing and Not-Agreeing (p . ∿q); (3) Not-Hearing and Not-Agreeing (∿p . ∿q); (4) Not-Hearing and Agreeing (∿p . q):

Hearing and Agreeing: This would represent successful communication, in that the hearer (in a speaker-hearer relationship) feels he understands what is being said and accepts it – with the status of *gbàgbọ́* – as part of his own store of information.

There seem to be different degrees of at least this variety of *gbàgbọ́*. The highest degree is expressed by *gbàgbọ́ jù*:

(24) It is the voice of the mouth [reference how convincing a person may be]. For example, when the *òyìnbọ́* said that he was going to my house that time, he did not know that I was inside [watching him saying it while he was just outside the house]. If he doesn't know that I saw him, if he returns back home [without coming inside], and when he sees me at another time, if I ask him whether he has been to my house, if he says he has not, we may begin to say this [i.e. to worry about his honesty because being just outside *is* regarded as a visit]. He may continue to say it – that he did not come. After some time he may say that he did come. But if I ask him and he answers me 'in one voice' and says that he did come, I will agree (*gbàgbọ́*) – more than that (*gbàgbọ́ jù*).

The word '*gbàgbọ́*' by itself – unmodified – signifies a 'normal' or 'average' degree. There seems to be at least one idiomatic expression for

---

[11] The noun form of *gbàgbó*.

less than normal. This is '*ò dá bí ẹ ni pe*', which the *oníṣẹ̀gùn* explain by:

(25) It means '*ó nrí bí eni yìi ṣe kìnì yí*' (it seems as if this person does this thing), but you did not see him do it. *They* say he did it.

Hearing and Not-Agreeing: This would be a situation in which the hearer feels he understands (*gbọ́*) what is being said but refuses to accept (*gbà*) that it is a correct or objective account. The most common example referred to by the *oníṣẹ̀gùn* is that of the person who is listening to a known liar (*irọ́*), though it is important to note the etm also translates this term as 'falsehood':

(26) But if you know that he is a liar (*eléke*), nobody will *gbàgbọ́* him. They will say, 'He tells lies'. They will not answer him.

(27) This is what a person does not do while people continue to say he did it. You can say that they tell lies against such a person.

Not-Hearing and Not-Agreeing: This would be a situation in which the hearer does not understand what is being said (including, it appears, by himself) and therefore cannot affirm or agree with it. The *oníṣẹ̀gùn* frequently refer to *iyè méjì* (which may be idiomatically rendered as 'of two minds' or 'two thoughts') when the hearer is confused about the correct interpretation to be placed upon what was said:

(28) Yesterday, when I told you to come here today, you agreed to accept (*gbàgbọ́*). But if I say again [on another occasion] that I've asked you to come, and if I come to think again that you will not come, this is *iyè méjì*. But as you have now come and I'm here for you, we both had *igbàgbọ́* [that we should come]. A person with *iyè méjì* is someone who does not know what he said yesterday. This means that he may not carry out the promise which he made yesterday.

(29) This is what we call *iyè méjì*. He has no *igbàgbọ́*.

(30) It means that your *ọkọ̀n* does not witness the thing – whether it is or is not. This is when you see something, but you are having two thoughts (*iyè méjì*) about it.

(31) If you hold something, do not take your hand away from it so as to hold another one. This is why *Ọlọ́run*[12] said we should ask for *igbàgbọ́* without *iyè méjì*. If the *ọkọ̀n* of a person moves like that and like this [gesture indicating back and forth; oscillation] . . ..

Not-hearing and Agreeing: The evidence supporting usage of the fourth of our logical possibilities is not as convincing. Perhaps the case of the fool, of the person who claims to have agreed and then makes statements that indicate he never understood in the first place, is a candidate:

---

[12]The supreme deity of the Yoruba.

(32) If a person is saying something, and if he goes on to say it like 'the word of animal', or the word of a foolish (*agò*) person, then people will come to say that 'that' is not how people should do things. 'That' is not how people usually say (*ẹ́ẹ ṣi bẹ́ẹ̀ kán an wí*). 'This' is how people usually say. If he is a real person, he will know that what he has done that time was not good.

As with *mọ̀*, *gbàgbọ́* is associated, or its locus is, with the *ọkọ̀n*. This is indicated by quotation 30, and by the following:

(33) If the *ẹmí*[13] of a person does not stay on something which he is taught, [even] if this [physical] ear hears, he cannot understand (*yé*). it. You know that the hearing is in the *ọkọ̀n*. When you use the ear to hear what they teach you, it goes into the *ọkọ̀n*.

As the *oníṣẹ̀gùn* refer only to the *ọkọ̀n* and not the *ẹrí ọkọ̀n*, we infer that the service it performs is not the same. A reasonable interpetation would be that as the person does not witness the information in a first-hand manner, the most he can judge or decide is whether he understands and (however tentatively) agrees to accept someone's words. He is not in a position to determine *òótọ́*.

The objects of *gbàgbọ́* – the things that one agrees to accept upon hearing them from someone – are the most difficult aspect of this complex term. It is easy enough to say 'anything that is second-hand', but once one recognizes that this may also include the whole of oral tradition, the analysis becomes potentially controversial. For it is oral tradition that has been stereotyped as the locus of *knowledge* in traditional cultures.

(34) We ourselves depend mainly upon *itàn* (etm: 'story'; 'history'). We will say that our fathers said this kind of thing has happened before. Those who are dead cannot *mọ̀* what is happening now. And we cannot *mọ̀* what they have done in the past ... You can only know the one you see with your own eyes.

(35) This is what you hear from other people. This is what you don't *mọ̀* but which you are saying. But if you don't hear it from people themselves, you cannot [should not] say it.[14]

(36) I say [mean] this [is something that] will happen. This means that something which 'our forefathers have been saying' is reliable (*ọ̀rọ̀ àgbà ṣẹ*). This is like a prophecy (*à sọ tẹ́lẹ̀*).[15]

(37) This is what you *gbọ́*. You may not understand it. You don't see it. But you *gbọ́* it.[16]

---

[13]See footnote 10 above.

[14-17]Each of these passages is meant to be an explanation of the following (in sequence) idioms used to signify an appeal to tradition: [14]'*àwon kan ńso wípé*'; [15]'*àwon baba ńlá wa máa nso*'; [16]'*agbọ́ wípé*'; and (next page) [17]'*àwon baba ńlá wa ni ó so èyí*'.

(38) This is an *àbí nibí* (etm: 'traditional') expression. This is what my father has been saying [as contrasted with my own 'seeing'] in my presence.[17]

The practical value of oral tradition, as in the passage above comparing it to a prophecy or prediction, is that it may contain solutions to problems that arise in the future:

(39) If you are a person who asks many questions [i.e. places a priority on collecting information], you may ask a word from someone and you will keep on asking from three to four [more] people. If they tell you, you will know it more than someone who keeps quiet. You will know what you want from the words of these three to four men who answered your question. You will have one or two words [ideas] from what the people told you. Anyday a question is asked about these things, you will find an answer [i.e. by recalling the solutions to similar problems that you've learned on the basis of your past 'questions'] which is similar to the answer [solution] you give.

We shall have more to say about the cross-cultural consequences of the Yoruba classifying oral tradition as *gbàgbó* rather than *mò* in the next two sections of this chapter.

A second, closely related object of *gbàgbó* is the information conveyed in the context of a so-called 'formal' education:

(40) This is really the knowledge of putting *ọkọ̀n* into something, which you go to school to learn. You know (*mò*) that your teachers don't come home with you. But when you get home and take your book and say, 'These are the things we learned today'. This is the same thing as '*Bayi ni àwọn baba ńlá wa sọ fún wa*' ('This is what our forefathers told us'). It is putting *ọkọ̀n* into things.

A third object of *gbàgbó* is so-called factual or 'book' information:

(41) In the past, when they taught you *oògùn* (etm: 'medicine'), or when an *itàn* (etm: 'story'; 'history') was told they put it 'inside' (*inú*[18]) [i.e. learned it]. It lived 'inside'. Whatever you are told as a story now, you put it 'inside' (*inú*) book [i.e. it is being written down]. And it will appear there [in the book] forever. There is no reason for another person to tell the story again. You just take the book and begin to read it.

A fourth, and by no means the least important, object of *gbàgbó* is the vast amount of information we take in from other people which we do not *mò* and which is not part of the established oral tradition. This may be what a friend tells us he did in Lagos last week, what we read in the daily newspaper, or what we hear on the radio.

Òótọ́ is firmly linked to *mò*. There is no equally firm correlate of *gbàgbó*

---

[17]See footnote 14, above.

[18]A term that is at least as complicated as *èmí*. See Hallen and Sodipo 1994. Here the idiomatic 'inside' must suffice if we are not to be led too far off the track of 'knowledge'-'belief'.

but there are several terms that are frequently associated with it. They are 'ọgbọ́n' (etm: 'wisdom'; 'sense') and 'òyé' (etm: 'understanding'; 'wisdom'; 'intelligence'):

(42) When you have a child you begin to teach him ọ́gbọ́n. When the father becomes old, then he will begin to say 'this' and 'this' are the things which they told us.

(43) This is what we call òyé. If a person is able to say what the elders (àgbà) have been saying for the past five years or ten years [i.e. oral tradition], the people who are there will say, 'This child (ọmọdé) has òyé'. It is òyé that we call ọgbọ́n, and àigbàgbé (etm: ?; 'not forgetting') and làákàyè (etm: ?; 'common-sense'). This is the something that makes you remember (rántí) all the things we have done.

We do not find it necessary to claim that gbàgbọ́ is the only context in which they occur, or that it is a sufficient condition of the only meanings they have.[19] We are only suggesting that it is at least significant that they do occur in the present context.

When igbàgbọ́ is challenged, àríyàn jiyàn (an argument) is again the likely consequence. *Verification* by means of empirical testing is a possibility, but we can now enlarge upon the circumstances outlined in the last section.

The speaker may lay claim to mọ̀, while the hearer(s) have reservations because they themselves did not witness the affair. If the speaker's imọ̀ involves some testable consequences, o ṣeéṣe/kò ṣeéṣe may be invoked. However, if the test confirms the speaker's imọ̀, the hearers would then say they too mọ̀ rather than that they gbàgbọ́. For they now have witnessed the thing themselves and are entitled to regard it as òótọ́.

A second possibility is that the speaker only lays claim to gbàgbọ́. If some significant form of testing is possible, and his igbàgbọ́ is confirmed, then all parties to the àríyàn jiyàn – speaker and hearer(s) – are entitled to regard the information as imọ̀.

If testing is *not* possible, if the only solution to an àríyàn jiyàn is by means of the *justification* of someone's claim, things become much more difficult. For then the argument must be resolved on the level of gbàgbọ́.

(44) If four people are talking, if the first says, 'I agree (gbà)', and the second and the third. But the fourth does not agree. We will ask him why he does not agree with this. And, if he agrees, this would mean that all of us have agreed. Then we shall say, 'Papọ̀' (etm 544: 'the word has come together'). But 'the word has not come together' when a person still disagrees.

---

[19]We say this because from other contextual associations it may be that ọgbọ́n and/or òye are the broader generic categories that sometimes contain *both* igbàgbọ́ and imọ̀ as species.

'The word comes together' when all the contesting parties agree and the dispute is settled. And what must happen if this is to obtain is that the various parties agree that they have reached the *nwádì* of the matter:

(45) This is an *àríyàn jiyàn*. People may ask them not to fight about this, but to go and find out from its *nwádì* (etm: ?; seek for base/bottom/cause/reason of the matter).

We suggest that *nwádì* is roughly equivalent to a correct understanding of the matter. But here again, one is unsure as to whether the proper formulation is that agreement automatically ensures that ('the' or 'a'?) correct understanding has been reached, or the reverse.

There are various routes to *nwádì*. To return to the possibility of the 'third person',[20] his having witnessed the *ìmò* of one of the contesting parties may be enough to convince the other(s) that they should *gbàgbó*.

A second route is to appeal to the *ìwà* (past public behaviour or moral 'character') of a speaker:

(46) Because I have been moving with someone, I know all his *ìwà*. I know what he could do and what he could not do. If another person should come and tell me that he does certain things, since I know his *ìwà* I know whether he can do it or not. I will *gbàgbó* that he does it. But if I do not know his *ìwà*, then I will say I do not *gbàgbó*.

(47) I *gbà ọ gbọ́* (*gbàgbọ́* you) when I *mò* your *ìwà*. But it is the one you see (*rí*) that is bigger [more convincing]. I see it with absolute certainty (*dájú dájú*) I *gbà ọ gbọ́* but I did not see the thing. But what I see clearly (*kedere*) I know with certainty (*dájú*).

(48) If thèy say someone did something, and if the second person says it is clear in his own eyes that the first person could not do such a thing, he will say, 'I *gbàgbọ́* he could not do such a thing'. Or he will say, 'I *gbàgbọ́* in that person, that he would not do such a thing'. Or he may say that, 'I *gbàgbọ́* he could do it'. This is [means] that he knows his *ìwà*.

(49) The difference between what I *mò* and what I *gbà* – the reason why you agree is that you have seen that thing or that the person who told you will never tell lies.

Obviously *ìwà* must also play an important role when a hearer is first assessing a speaker's claims to either *ìmò* or *ìgbàgbó*. But the *oníṣẹ̀gùn* make specific reference to it more frequently when a claim to *gbàgbó* is disputed. (After all, even liars (*elékè*) may often tell the truth.) The important point, however, is that an appeal to *ìwà* – if successful – cannot produce *ìmò*. It can at best end in *ìgbàgbó* (for the hearer(s)).

A third route is the use of plain, unmitigated *àlàyé* (explanation). But the

---

[20]See page 63 above.

circumstances under which a hearer may ask a speaker to *ṣé àlàyé* also vary. First, without necessarily casting aspersions on the speaker's character (who, by the way, is also judging the hearer's character), the hearer may honestly feel that he has not understood what the other person was saying ('Not-Hearing and Not-Agreeing'):

> (50) If you are telling me something now, if you say everything without any stop and I don't understand what you are telling me, I will say, '*Ṣé àlàyé* how this matter starts'. It is then you will tell me, line by line. If you are sending me on an errand, it is then that I will understand what you are asking me to do.

Such a positive result is somewhat optimistic, for the speaker may deliberately choose to give a *bad* explanation:

> (51) There are bad (*burúkú*) explanations. If I want to deceive you, I will give you bad explanations. If I don't want to deceive you, I will make good explanations for you. If I explain good things to you, it means I like (*fẹ̀ràn*) you. If I want to deceive you, the explanation which I want to give you will not be good. Since you don't know whether what I'm saying is good or bad, these are the two types of explanations [bad and good; deceptive and non-deceptive].

It is not clear that a bad explanation *necessarily* implies a bad character (*iwà*). Error, incompetence, and perhaps even morally justifiable deceit are also possible. *Ìwà* could only become relevant to the degree that it is possible to infer and condemn motives from past behaviour.

In any case, even if the speaker gives the best explanation he can, and the hearer listens as carefully as *he* can, it is still possible that the affair will end in a stalemate. The situation is still one of *àríyàn jiyàn*. In such cases the recommendation of the *oníṣẹ̀gùn* is as eloquent as it is realistic:

> (52) This may come out when we are arguing (*iyàn jíjà*). If we are trying to know the 'bottom' (*nwádi*) – if the words of three people are together and those of two [other] people are different, the words have not come together. If their words are not together, the only thing we can do is to be patient (*sùrù*) and to start looking for another 'bottom' of it.

8. Relations and Comparisons Between 'Mọ̀' and 'Gbàgbọ́'

It seems a safe generalization to say that the *oníṣẹ̀gùn* link *mọ̀* to first-hand or direct experience, and *gbàgbọ́* to second-hand experience or testimony. Hence, when a father passes on his own *ìmọ̀* to a son, if it is something to which the son is not *himself* a witness, it is received (by him) as *igbàgbọ́*. This may be exemplified by completing the passage that was partially quoted above (42):

(53) When you have a child you begin to teach him wisdom (*lọgbọ́n*). When the father becomes old, then he will begin to say 'this' and 'this' are the things which they told us. Whatever he has seen or heard, he will be saying [passing along] the same thing to his son. But the son has not seen all this. Whatever we have not seen but of which we are told is what we call 'this' and 'this' are the things they told us.

It also appears reasonable to conclude that information obtained on the basis of *mọ̀* has a significantly greater degree of certitude (e.g. *dájú* as used on page 70 above) than information obtained on the basis of *gbàgbọ́*:

(54) You will see that you use your own eyes to see (*rí*) it – that it is *òótọ́*. You should not have two thoughts of it.

It is possible for information obtained on the basis of *gbàgbọ́* to become *mọ̀*. A father may tell his son of a certain procedure to follow when faced with a certain problem. But it is not until the son actually puts his father's suggestion to the test and has the opportunity to see it for himself and have it witnessed by his *okọ̀n* that it *may* (it may fail the test) become *imọ̀* for him. This also highlights the importance of testing. As the system has been expounded, there is virtually no margin for *imọ̀* that has not been empirically confirmed.

* * * *

What is most intriguing is the degree to which this epistemological system (arising from the conditions of *mọ̀* and *gbàgbọ́*) differs from the supposed model of traditional epistemological systems – systems of information that incorporate a significant element of oral tradition. That model is itself somewhat controversial, for there are those who maintain that it is only incidentally empirical and instrumental in character (Beattie 1966a) and those who argue that it is, though not to a degree that makes it characteristically critical or objective (Horton 1967).

Those who defend the first alternative argue that analysing such a system *as if* it were structurally somehow scientifically empirical overlooks the symbolic, poetic, expressive, and magical elements that constitute its most distinguishing characteristics. The ritual elements of such information systems are there precisely because the people do not have the requisite empirical expertise at hand to do for themselves – on the empirical level – what needs to be done. Hence they *express* their desire that it be done in a symbolic form.

The second alternative argues for the essentially theoretical character of traditional thought. In other words, it really is meant to explain, predict and control events in the empirical world. But its character is flawed by the fact that the established theories are assigned 'an absolute and exlcusive validity'.

> Much has been made of the scientist's essential scepticism toward established beliefs; and one must, I think, agree that this above all is what distinguishes him from the traditional thinker. (Horton: 168)

> This underlying readiness to scrap or demote established theories on the ground of poor predictive performance is perhaps the most important single feature of the scientific attitude. (Horton: 169)

> One theory is judged better than another with explicit reference to its efficacy in explanation and prediction. (Horton: 164)

Once a traditional theory has been developed it tends to remain in force indefinitely, and to undergo insignificant change. Often the members of the culture concerned can do nothing but appeal *to* tradition ('We believe it because the forefathers believed it.'), when asked to explain or to defend the theory. 'Causal accounts are not worth giving for the beliefs of individuals who have simply been taught what their social group holds.' (Peel 1969: 71) Consequently the identification, abstraction and analysis of the structural elements and characteristics of theoretical systems, of explanations, tends to be relatively underdeveloped:

> traditional thought has tended to get on with the work of explanation, without pausing for reflection upon the nature or rules of this work.
> (Horton: 162)

Each of the above alternatives has generated considerable controversy and opposition – from the other and from external sources.[21] Our concern is not so much in adding to this debate as it is in trying to understand *why* our own model of a Yoruba theoretical system has come to be *so* much at variance with all of the above. For we have outlined a system that is more reflective, more theoretically attuned, more sceptical, and more empirical than had previously been entertained.

The refrain, 'What you are told may not be true', is so profoundly associated by the Yoruba with the *mọ̀-gbàgbọ́* distinction that it is clear they have learned it from 'experience' and do regard it as applicable to oral tradition. Given the added conditions that *imọ̀* must be seen for oneself, and that *igbàgbọ́* (which includes tradition) cannot qualify as *imọ̀* unless one does, the evidence supporting an uncritical attitude towards tradition is no longer convincing.

However, before we are tempted into drawing sweeping comparisons or

---

[21]See Horton 1960; Goody 1961; Beattie 1966b; Horton 1967; Turner 1967; Goody and Watt 1968; Peel 1969; Pratt 1972; Horton and Finnegan 1973; Gellner 1970; Skorupski 1976; Goody 1977; Marwick 1973; Wiredu 1980; Hallen and Sodipo 1994.

conclusions, our own approach may be open to challenge for its own inadequacies. These must be weighed before we begin to take for granted the objectivity of our results. The most obvious is that our reporting of the *oníṣẹ̀gùn* is not representative. Either we have misinterpreted the significance of their remarks or our remarks during the course of the discussions persuaded them to speak in a manner in which they would not ordinarily.

We would argue against either of these alternatives. We have quoted them at length (see also Appendix) and so frequently to demonstrate that we are accurately conveying their viewpoint. Furthermore, they are men who are distinguished in their profession and relatively prominent in their community. They are no one's fool and cannot be enticed or misled into making pronouncements on subjects of which they are ignorant.

A second possibility would be that they have somehow been touched or influenced by a 'scientific' attitude or outlook that is not indigenous. This we also would reject. None of these men have undergone formal education or speak the English language. Consequently there is no significant avenue by means of which such influence could have been conveyed.

A third possible failing would be that, as the *oníṣẹ̀gùn* constitute a professional 'elite' in Yoruba society, it is misleading to take their viewpoint as generally representative of the society and its attitudes towards tradition, etc. If we had been encouraging them to speak specifically *as oníṣẹ̀gùn*, this complaint could be legitimate. But in the majority of the quoted passages they are deliberately endeavouring to report ordinary usage – to explain the attitudes of the average person towards the information he possesses.

A fourth possibility would be that our presentation of *mọ̀* and *gbàgbọ́* and the relations between them is not representative because we place an emphasis upon certain components of the 'system' that is different from that assigned to them by either the *oníṣẹ̀gùn or* the average Yoruba. For example, because we have been conditioned to appreciate the value of empirical testing and verification, we seize upon and inflate the few vague references to it in the *oníṣẹ̀gùn*'s remarks and inflate their significance far beyond what was ever intended.

It is more difficult to make a convincing reply to this criticism than the others. We beg indulgence to delay the attempt until we have had the chance to take account of the next and final criticism. This has two parts: that actions speak louder than words, and that form cannot be adequately treated independently of content. The first part would argue that the greatest limitation to our methodology is the disproportionate emphasis placed upon how people describe and explain what they do. Virtually no account is taken of comparing this with behaviour. It might therefore be the case that the emphasis placed upon the empirical by the remarks of the *oníṣẹ̀gùn* would be repudiated by their actions. For example, they may describe themselves as willing to declare hypotheses false, but practice would show that they have constant recourse to secondary elaboration.

The second 'part' would argue that it is, to put it politely, misleading to exaggerate the empirical and sceptical *form* of a system of information that permits, as component beliefs, things like incantations, witchcraft and a host of spiritual forces and powers. A truly empirical and/or sceptical system of information would have singled out and dispensed with such unempirical elements.

Let us first deal with 'actions speak louder than words', and suggest it should be reformulated as 'words should speak as loud as actions'. To the best of our knowledge there are virtually no published studies of the Yoruba conceptual system from an analytic point of view.[22] Why is this? We would suggest that it is in some measure a consequence of the stereotype referred to above. For there is a feeling that there cannot be much of analytical interest or importance to find in a conceptual system that is 'traditional' (e.g. magical, insignificantly critical, etc.) in nature. But surely it is important to appreciate the perspectives the Yoruba themselves take upon what they are doing, particularly when we discover a much greater and more explicit emphasis on elements like the hypothetical, the empirical and the critical than had heretofore been imagined.

In the quoted passages the *oníṣẹ̀gùn* introduce numerous concrete examples (including many that obviously did happen or are happening in the room where the discussion is taking place). These are still in the form of 'words', but they are about as close as one can get to picturing actions with them. What is more important, however, is that they take the accounts of the *oníṣẹ̀gùn* well beyond the realm of epistemological or methodological platitudes. They provide action-oriented illustrations of a methodology intrinsic in the criteria of these two concepts.

As for form versus content, there already is an interesting, ongoing debate on this issue (Horton 1967; Gellner 1970; Hallen and Sodipo 1994). All we should like to add here is that it is possible for the social scientist to place *too much* emphasis upon a belief in incantations or in witchcraft. To refer again to the examples of the *oníṣẹ̀gùn*, it is clear that the information system also contains a large amount of theoretical elements and relations that are non-'magical'. It is important that the *oníṣẹ̀gùn* do not find it necessary to refer to 'magical' elements when elucidating the conditions of *mọ̀*

---

[22]See Sodipo 1973 and Abimbola and Hallen 1993.

and *gbàgbó*. (From previous discussions we are convinced that this is not because they were cautious or secretive about making reference to such things.)

To come finally to the objection that this account may be guilty of ethnocentric emphases upon individual theoretical elements: it is an account of a theoretical *system* as well as of its component elements. Testing does not occur in isolation. It occurs as one possibility when there is a controversial information claim. We feel that the importance we have assigned to testing in our own analyses reflects the importance assigned to it in the remarks of the *oníṣẹ̀gùn* relative to other theoretical elements (*òótọ́, àlàyé, iwà, ọgbọ́n, papọ̀, gbàgbọ́,* etc.).

We therefore feel that this presentation of a Yoruba theoretical system is representative and should at least have the consequence of making the academic fieldworker take another look at how these criteria may work out in practice. The system that this chapter presents in outline form *is* radically different from the model assumed appropriate to traditional cultures. If that difference is not a consequence of our faulty methodology, then it represents what the *oníṣẹ̀gùn* really do think. If so, it is extremely important to pay careful attention to how *they* apply *this*[23] system in practice.

9. Comparisons of the 'Knowledge'–'Belief' Distinction with the 'Mọ̀'–'Gbàgbọ́' Distinction

The *oníṣẹ̀gùn* do not explicitly identify varieties of *mọ̀* that are immediately comparable to 'knowing that', 'knowing how', etc. However this does not mean that it is impossible to say the equivalent of '*Mo mọ̀* that' or *Mo mọ̀* how' in Yoruba.

It is possible to identify several varieties – or perhaps levels – of *mọ̀* indirectly, by means of *òótọ́*. Certainly the relationships between 'know' and 'true' and between '*mọ̀*' and '*òótọ́*' seem remarkably similar. Both indicate epistemologic certainty and both apparently express a correspondence between what is known/*mọ̀* and whatever actually is/was the case. From the quotation on page 62 above, it appears that *òótọ́* is only different in that it may apply *both* to a certain kind of experience and *also* to propositions recounting that experience. An English-language speaker would not normally describe experience as 'true'. 'True' is a term reserved for propositions.

---

[23]Without immediately importing alien notions of meaningful behaviour, scientific method, functional relevance, or even of 'common' sense.

When casting about for English-language equivalents, if one considers the conditions of *mọ̀* (*rí* + *ẹ̀rí ọkọ̀n*) and couples these with the usages of *òótọ́*, it appears that the most accurate model would be a combination of 'knowledge by acquaintance' and 'knowledge that'. The English-language conditions of knowledge by acquaintance were sufficient first-hand experience of something so that the person could recognize it again. This first-hand element is certainly compatible with the conditions of *mọ̀*. Furthermore, in the Yoruba system it is only when I have made the acquaintance of a thing that I am entitled to claim that I *mọ̀* something of it in propositional form ('knowledge that'). (If the first-hand element is lacking, the appropriate term would be *gbàgbọ́*.) This means that for the Yoruba it is impossible to have the equivalent of 'knowledge that' of something one has not 'known by acquaintance'. Or the other way round, 'knowledge by acquaintance' is a prerequisite to (or condition of) 'knowledge that'. On the other hand, in the English-language system the role of testimony or *second*-hand information in 'knowledge that' is enormously important. In English, knowledge by acquaintance is not a sufficient condition of knowledge that. This will shortly become a key element in our comparison of the two systems.

Knowledge – Ìmọ̀

	Knowledge by	Knowledge 'That'
YORUBA	Acquaintance ⟶	(derived from first-
	(first-hand)	hand experience)

	Testimony	Knowledge 'That'
ENGLISH	(second-hand ⟶	(derived from second-
	experience)	hand experience)

We used the term 'correspondence' just above, and the Yoruba system does display elements of Correspondence theory. Statements recounting *imọ̀* are presumed to correspond to what one has seen and comprehended. But there does not seem to be a Yoruba equivalent of *the right of birth and ancient possession*. This was said to provide a *prima facie* justification for the 'traditional knowledge' a man imbibes but does not explicitly verify simply by virtue of being the member of a certain society. As we have remarked, such 'knowledge' would be classified in the Yoruba system as *igbàgbọ́*. The role of testimony (of second-hand information) on the level of *imọ̀* is not significant.

In practice it does seem to be the case that a person is most often called upon to jusify his claim to *mọ̀* when it is challenged. Perhaps it therefore is appropriate to hypothesize a Yoruba Principle of Charity *on the level of mọ̀*. For it would be unrealistic to presume the system requires the verification of *every* claim to knowledge, *all* the time.

*Verification of Knowledge/*Imọ̀

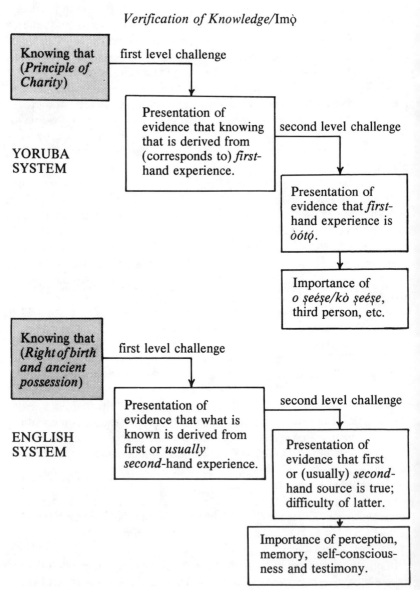

It is not clear whether *mò* is regarded as the equivalent of a private mental state or whether it is dispositional or whether it may be both. More detailed study and analysis of the psychology and physiology underlying the Yoruba epistemology would be required.

Comparisons between the varieties of 'believe' and '*gbàgbó*' also are possible on a selective basis. Since the *iwà* of a speaker may always be a consideration, the most accurate English-language model would be a combination of 'believing a person' and 'believing that'. In English either is subject to degrees and in Yoruba, as we have suggested, so would be the equivalent of their combination. A person's willingness to *gbàgbó* what someone is saying is a function of how sure that person is of the speaker's *iwà*.

If our four 'logical' varieties of *gbàgbó* are representative, then the latter two ('Not-Hearing and Not-Agreeing' and 'Not-Hearing and Agreeing') characterize negative *gbàgbó* – situations in which there is no *gbàgbó*. And the second variety ('Hearing and Not-Agreeing') is appropriate to a situation where the hearer makes a negative assessment of a speaker's character and so refuses to *gbàgbó* what he says.

The *onísègùn* do not articulate a subsidiary usage of *gbàgbó* that could be equivalent to 'believing in' – to an absolute, degreeless conviction or commitment to another person or creed. Nor would it be helpful to suggest that this may be found on the level of *mò*. A hearer can *mò* the *igbàgbó* of another only if he can see and witness it for himself. The element of 'faith', of 'trust' in an external source, is no longer there.

Does *gbàgbó* function as a propositional attitude? If our 'figurative' rendering of it into English ('agreeing to accept what one *hears* from someone') is acceptable, then clearly what speakers say and listeners 'hear' are prospositions. It is when one compares believe and *gbàgbó* with reference to their objects, the classes of propositions towards which they may *be* attitudes, that the significant differences occur:

CATEGORIES OF INFORMATION

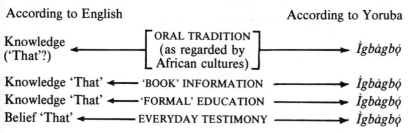

According to English		According to Yoruba
Knowledge ('That'?) ←	⎡ ORAL TRADITION ⎤ (as regarded by ⎣ African cultures) ⎦ →	*Ìgbàgbó*
Knowledge 'That' ←	'BOOK' INFORMATION →	*Ìgbàgbó*
Knowledge 'That' ←	'FORMAL' EDUCATION →	*Ìgbàgbó*
Belief 'That' ←	EVERYDAY TESTIMONY →	*Ìgbàgbó*

We have previously remarked upon the erroneous English-language model that insists African propositional attitudes towards oral traditions are best translated as the equivalents of 'knowledge'. We also pointed out that, as the Yoruba regard the contents of 'book' information and 'formal' education as extensions or relations of oral tradition, they also are classified as *igbàgbọ́*. Therefore it is apparently only with reference to the status of 'everyday' testimony that the two systems agree.

In English, verification or justification of belief is usually called for when it has been challenged. Otherwise a Principle of Charity is implicitly operative. In Yoruba *àríyàn jiyàn* also effectively represents a challenge. We therefore suggest that it is reasonable to hypothesize a parallel Principle of Charity.

We find an interesting difference in emphasis between the two systems when it comes to the justification of belief. The Yoruba system of *àlàyé* (explanation) strikes us as much more listener-oriented. In the English-language system the primary emphasis is upon the speaker's justifying his belief by means of appeals to other beliefs or to *prima facie* evidence derived from perception, memory, etc. In the Yoruba system all participants to a debate are *explicitly* called upon to provide whatever relevant *igbàgbọ́* and information they may possess, and all are *explicitly* called upon to judge the outcome.

Again, it is not possible to make any determinate decision with reference to whether *gbàgbọ́* is used to indicate a disposition, a private 'mental' state or some combination of the two. More research and analysis is required.

We have now reached a point where it is possible to compare the English (know–believe) and Yoruba (*mọ̀–gbàgbọ́*) *systems*. Let us first deal with the obvious similarities: (1) there is *some*thing first-hand about know and *mọ̀*, and second-hand about believe and *gbàgbọ́*, in both systems; (2) there is greater certitude attached to know and *mọ̀* than to believe and *gbàgbọ́*, in both systems; (3) it is possible for information that is belief and *igbàgbọ́* to become knowledge and *imọ̀*, in both systems.

We previously suggested that the English-language system is three-tiered. We would say the same for the Yoruba one, though the content of each tier is different:

MỌ̀	GBÀGBỌ́	
(1) Mọ̀ ⟶ (best)	(2) Gbàgbọ́ that may ⟶ be verified (*o ṣeéṣe/kò ṣeéṣe*) (second best)	(3) Gbàgbọ́ that may only be justified (*àlàyé*) (third best)

Gbàgbọ́ that may be verified is gbàgbọ́ that may become mọ̀. Gbàgbọ́ that is not open to verification (testing) and must therefore be evaluated on the basis of justification (àlàyé, papọ̀, etc.) cannot become mọ̀ and consequently its òótọ́ must remain indeterminate.

The point of difference between the two systems that we find to be of greatest significance is the relative role of testimony or second-hand information. In the Yoruba system any information conveyed on the basis of testimony is, until verified, igbàgbọ́. In the English system a vast amount of information conveyed on the basis of testimony is, without verification, classified as 'knowledge that'. Much of the latter is information that the individual concerned would not even know *how* to verify. Yet it is still 'knowledge that'.

How ironic, then, that the model of African thought systems produced by English-language culture should typify them as systems that treat second-hand information (oral tradition, 'book' knowledge, etc.) as though it were true, as though it were knowledge! This is precisely what the Yoruba epistemological system, as outlined above, outspokenly and adamantly refuses to do. But the English-language epistemological system does – grossly. Therefore it, in the end, fits its own model for traditional thought systems better than Yoruba ever can!

10. Final Comments on the Transitional Indeterminacy of Propositional Attitudes

In this paper we have been describing and analysing Yoruba terms with English-language meanings. This is a practice about which Quine would have serious reservations, unless one is prepared to acknowledge the accompanying indeterminacy. This, to a degree, we are prepared to do. But we shall argue, *contra* Quine, that our translations of Yoruba propositional attitudes into the English language are *sufficiently* determinate to demonstrate that such 'attitudes' are not universal.

A preliminary consideration should be whether one is justified in regarding mọ̀ and gbàgbọ́ as propositional attitudes *in the Yoruba language*. The etm may translate them as such, but does our own data and analysis confirm this? (More extreme would be to ask whether the category 'propositional attitude' need be universal.) We feel that sufficient evidence is presented in this chapter to support the common association of these two terms with propositions in a manner closely resembling their English-language counterparts. (Though we also noted that mọ̀ may have experience as well as propositions as its object.)

What we dispute with Quine is the *degree* of indeterminacy 'infecting' our English-language translations of the Yoruba meanings underlying these two terms. We shall do this first on the level of the criteria governing their usage, and secondly on the level of their objects.

The association of *rí* (visual perception) with *mọ̀* is constant, and the identification of its behavioural meaning a fairly straightforward matter. The association of *èrí ọkọ̀n* with *mọ̀* is also constant, but it appears highly theoretical in content and therefore resistant to straightforward empirical or behavioural definition. Our translation of it as 'comprehension' plus 'judgement' is therefore contentious. Indeed, the fact that we propose this as a better interpretation than the etm's 'conscience' supports Quine's argument that alternative, cogent translations of standing sentences are possible.

The association of the *absence* of *rí* with *gbàgbọ́* is constant and its behavioural manifestation fairly straightforward. The association of 'what one is told' with *gbàgbọ́* is also constant and its behavioural manifestations significantly empirical in character. Final treatment of this last point must be deferred until we consider the objects of *gbàgbọ́* below.

Assessing the empirical status of the *objects* of *mọ̀* and *gbàgbọ́* may also help to make their translations into English-language meanings more determinate. With reference to *mọ̀*, most of its objects will be observation sentences. Establishing this will not make its translation by the English-language 'know', in particular, determinate. (We shall shortly suggest that the insistence on single word equivalents between languages may sometimes do more harm than good.) But putting a cluster of relatively empirically verifiable meanings constantly associated with *mọ̀* into reasonably determinate English translation does serve to make the dimensions and limits of the term *more* determinate than before.

With reference to *gbàgbọ́*, it would appear possible to demonstrate on empirical grounds that oral tradition (via the idiomatic expressions that serve as verbal signs[24]), formal education, and 'book' information, at least, are its objects. This again would serve to make its dimensions more determinate than before.

To come to the matter of single word equivalents in translation, we have deliberately avoided this form of translation for either term. We do not affirm the etm's 'know' and we do not propose an alternative. We feel that 'know' is more confusing than helpful (since both criteria and objects differ between the two language systems), and we are not able to provide a less

---

[24]See footnotes 14-17 above.

misleading English-language alternate. We have therefore preferred to *transliterate mọ̀* into the English language (e.g. 'I *mọ̀* that you came to see me').

With *gbàgbọ́* our practice is slightly different. Again, we do not affirm the English 'believe' as a representative rendering. But we do at one point propose an alternative: 'agreeing to accept what someone says'. Quine could point to this as evidence of translation indeterminacy, and to an extent we would agree. But if we had not gone beyond reducing the term to its two components ('accept' + 'hear'), if we had not done something, admittedly hypothetical, to weaken the reader's association of it with the etm's 'believe', he would have had difficulty following the direction our analysis was about to take. In any case, once the translations of criteria and objects are taken into account and their empirically determinate content weighed, we feel that our awkward rendering of this difficult term *is* more representative. There is still a 'gap' between empirical content and assigned theoretical meaning, but it is not *so* indeterminate:

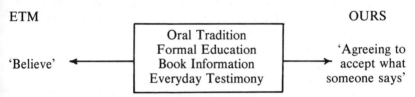

ETM		OURS
'Believe' ◄─────	Oral Tradition Formal Education Book Information Everyday Testimony	─────► 'Agreeing to accept what someone says'

Even so, for the most part we also transliterate *gbàgbọ́* into English, leaving it to be defined by its criteria and objects.

We do not feel that we have provided perfectly determinate translations of either '*mọ̀*' or '*gbàgbọ́*'. But when compared with what had existed to date, we feel that our accounts are considerably *more* determinate. This is due primarily to the special attention devoted to the empirical conditions and content of each term. We would be pleased if the response to this chapter generates information about additional empirical content that may lead to even more determinate translations. All of this is possible because empirical controls and evidence are in some cases sufficient to determine whether one translation of a theoretical term (or standing sentence) is an improvement on another.

Quine would probably argue that *transliteration* is a rather naive way of postponing the inevitable. The indeterminacy the translator must cope with on the level of criteria and objects may be no less than that on the level of the original terms. If it is not – if it *is* less – then the 'gap' between content, etc. and an intellectual abstraction like 'believe' is still enormous, leaving the latter open to alternate interpretations. One may worry over empirical 'contents' *ad infinitum*. One may squeeze criteria of every drop of behavioural reference. The margin that remains is *still* unmanageable when it comes to providing a final translation.

We disagree, and suggest that the analyses presented in this chapter justify that disagreement. Theoretical translation is extremely difficult but it is not *so* radically indeterminate. Neither is it totally determinate. It falls somewhere in between, and may vary with the term. Nevertheless there are guidelines to follow. There are measures to take which may provide a clearer indication of alien theoretical meaning in the language of translation.

11. Conclusion

The alien who refers to a bilingual dictionary and relies upon its single term equivalents will likely presume that the objects and conditions of the two terms are the same. One is therefore led to wonder how frequent the occasions are on which one may find a Yoruba speaking English words but assigning them Yoruba-language criteria and objects ('meanings'), or the reverse? And how serious the consequent misunderstandings may be?

In this chapter we feel that we have made a case for the following:

(1) That certain techniques may be borrowed from the philosophical 'school' known as conceptual analysis and utilized with value in cross-cultural, conceptual comparisons.

(2) That indeterminacy on the level of theoretical translation is a serious problem. However there are measures that may be taken to reduce it to a level where significant determinate translation of theory becomes possible.

(3) That the analyses and comparisons made between 'know' and '*mọ̀*' and between 'believe' and '*gbàgbọ́*' demonstrate that their meanings are significantly different.

(4) That these differences are sufficient to justify our concluding that propositional attitudes are not universal. It is therefore hazardous to take the propositional attitudes of one language as paradigms for the propositional attitudes of other languages.

(5) That the conceptual systems of alien languages – including those of so-called 'traditional' cultures – have implicit in them alternative epistemological, metaphysical, moral, etc. systems that are of philosophical interest in their own right.

(6) That these conclusions are incomplete (not indeterminate!). Many interesting comparisons between the two systems as presented remain to be made, but considerations of time and space force us to conclude at this point.

3. The Secrecy of the 'Àjé'

The witch-doctor (a title often misapplied) is a person who seeks to doctor and cure those who are believed to have been bewitched. He is honoured and works in public, whereas the witch is supposed to work in secret and is greatly feared.
Geoffrey Parrinder (1970: 15)

1. Introduction

Few subjects have been more misunderstood than witchcraft.
Geoffrey Parrinder (1970: 10)

A substantial part of the mystery surrounding witches derives from the veil of secrecy behind which they live and practise their 'art'. Any attempt to understand witchcraft must penetrate this veil and at the same time appreciate the reasons for its existence. In what follows we hope to take a more careful look at witchcraft as a cross-cultural phenomenon than was possible during our previous discussion of Evans-Pritchard.[1] At that time our concern was to question whether and to what extent his analyses and translations of Zande witchcraft could be affected by the indeterminacy thesis.

We shall not bother to restate Quine's arguments or to apply them in an explicit manner to the other sources we are about to consider. Nevertheless Quine's stubbornly persistent caution and scepticism with reference to the ease of finding theoretical meaning equivalents are meant to carry over as important guiding elements in the substratum or background to the more pedestrian analyses of this chapter. For whether discussing the writings of a theologian, a historian, an anthropologist, or a psychologist, witchcraft is invariably treated as a kind of cultural universal that may occur in any society.

Because of this our initial concern will be to discuss various Western models of the witchcraft phenomenon (with interest centering upon the *personality* of the witch), and to evaluate them as explanatory devices when applied to non-Western behaviour. We shall then be in a position to determine to what extent this kind of approach may help or hinder the

[1]See above pp.26–29.

explication of a theoretical concept like '*àjé*', the supposed Yoruba equivalent of the English-language 'witch'.

One final introductory note: in our analyses comparatively little emphasis will be placed upon the phantasy symbolism associated with the witchcraft phenomenon – such things as the colour black, flying (on broomsticks, etc.) at night, and the eating of children. Our central interest in 'witch' is as a possible *personality-type*. We shall therefore concentrate upon more behaviourally determinate actions, such as whether the witch is in general regarded as aggressive, mentally ill, of superior intelligence, and so forth.

2. Analyses of Western Witchcraft

If one undertakes a survey of the literature dealing with the peak of the witchcraft phenomenon in sixteenth- and seventeenth-century Europe, the religious, the historical, the sociological/anthropological and the psychological are among the most prominent methodological viewpoints to be taken into account. One element common to many of these studies is a kind of cultural embarrassment. The authors, who can be considered as Westerners, are often amazed, even embarrassed, by the fact that thousands of accused 'witches' were persecuted, tortured, imprisoned, and sometimes executed for 'crimes' that clearly exceeded the powers of any normal or even abnormal human being. Consequently the period of the witchcraft phenomenon is regarded as one of the last, embarrassingly sensational, 'primitive' antecedents of the 'modern' Western era. It may be of primarily historical interest (today) to study and to attempt to understand it as it was, but witchcraft ceased to be any kind of significant cultural element in Western society hundreds of years ago.

Among specialists on the Western witchcraft phenomenon are those who defend the persecution of witches as a legitimate enterprise because witchcraft is, quite literally, true. It is an evil, spiritually directed heresy that poses a deliberate threat to any established social order. 'Anthropology alone offers no explanation of witchcraft. Only the trained theologian can adequately treat the subject.' (Summers 1973: 45) Today this Christian, 'literalist' approach is perhaps less in intellectual fashion than others. It is also of less interest to us insofar as it allows for the literal truth of much of the phantasy symbolism (the pact with the Devil, for example). Nevertheless it at least deserves mention because it sees witchcraft as a universal human problem that has 'a permanent and invaried character', and the witch as a person who is quintessentially evil (*the* applicable spiritual category), antisocial, hostile and deliberately malicious to other people.

One of the most scrupulous and imaginative contemporary studies of the Western witchcraft phenomenon (in sixteenth- and seventeenth-century England) is Thomas's *Religion and the Decline of Magic*. He is described as a social historian and his analyses are three-dimensional: conceptual, sociological, and psychological. In what follows we may reclassify something as 'conceptual' that Thomas would prefer to regard as 'sociological'. This does not mean that we regard his own classifications as mistaken. Rather that, as philosphers, our understanding of 'conceptual' is somewhat broader than his own.

Conceptual. What is of particular interest in Thomas's work is that he endeavours to grapple with the conceptual apparatus of the lower classes as much as with that of the higher. Unlike ecclesiastical and judicial authorities (for whom all witches were dangerous, anti-social elements), members of the lower class generally made a distinction between so-called 'cunning men/women' (or 'white' or 'good' witches, or wizards) and genuinely malevolent, anti-social witches. The task of the 'good' witch was to help the victim of malevolent witchcraft. They were therefore rarely punished, though heavily patronized, and, for their own protection from higher authority, rather secretive.

According to Thomas the essence of malevolent witchcraft was the ability 'to inflict damage by occult means'. (1973: 531) The important operative term here is 'occult', which he explains as the power 'to mysteriously [non-naturally] injure other people'. The injury was usually a physical one, either to the individual or to his property, and was supposedly achieved by the use of such magical techniques as (magical) physical contact, cursing, and the use of wax images.

As for the explanatory function of witchcraft:

> In a society technologically more backward than ours the immediate attraction of the belief in witchcraft is not difficult to understand. It served as a means of accounting for the otherwise inexplicable misfortunes of daily life. (Thomas 1973: 638)

Witchcraft was the explanation to be used when no other was forthcoming. Furthermore it was a type of explanation that provided for the victims doing something concrete about their misfortunes. They could consult a cunning man, obtain (magical) remedies, and hopefully even identify and prosecute the responsible malevolent person.

Sociological. Two points are of particular interest under this heading. By the first, one is again made to appreciate the importance Thomas attaches to understanding witchcraft from the viewpoint of the lower classes. Under the previous subheading we discussed the function of the witchcraft belief for the victim. Here we must take into account its importance for the witch.

In general witches came from the lowest ranks of society. It was this class that suffered most from the poverty, the desperation, the frustration and the helplessness that are consequent to economic and political impotence. Rather than succumbing to resignation and self-pity, assuming the role of the witch offered such hopelessly downtrodden individuals some hope of power and vengeance, even if ultimately illusory.

Secondly, in the lower classes the position of women relative to men was weaker, making them comparatively more susceptible. Therefore, although it was usually said that men could become witches as easily as women, the overwhelming majority of accusations were made against women. No doubt many were innocent. But it may also follow that more women than men intentionally embraced witchcraft as some means towards mitigating their misery.

Psychological. In discussing this dimension we shall go somewhat beyond the bounds of Thomas's own analysis. This is because on both the individual and social levels modern psychology has come to be regarded as the most promising source of an objective explanation for the phenomenon. However, precisely because psychology is 'modern', it is difficult to certify any existent psychological analysis as definitive. All must be speculative in nature because no adequate *clinical* study of Western witchcraft was possible in its own historical period. And to date no account of Western witchcraft written *by a witch* has been uncovered that is not a confession, that is, that was given freely rather than consequent to the threat or application of social, ecclesiastical or judicial sanctions.

According to Thomas, in the broadest sense witchcraft as an explanatory device seems to have offered a degree of psychological release and reassurance. It provided the 'victim' of misfortune with an explanation for it, and with a plan of action to redress it. It provided the 'witches', viewing themselves as victims of social, economic and political oppression, with an avenue of protest belief and action.

Social psychologists try to explain what it means if a society produces witches and to identify the 'stress' points and situations in which they are more likely to occur. (Kiev 1964: 24) But it is clinical psychologists, in particular, who treat the Western witch as a disturbed personality and who hypothesize analyses that make reference to depression, neurosis, hysterical and psychosomatic illness, and auto-suggestion. Even Thomas suggests that the phenomenon may also be interpreted as a manifestation of mental illness because it did not always work for the psychological benefit of the witch. Many 'witches' may have confessed to ghastly and patently impossible crimes because, as lower class outcasts, they had become overwhelmed by their own sense of worthlessness and were suffering from severe depression.

We shall return to this important clinical dimension of the Western witchcraft phenomenon when undertaking the comparisons of witchcraft in the West with witchcraft in Africa. For the moment it is to be noted and, given the historical limitations, its speculative and controversial character emphasized.

The third and last authority we shall turn to for a model of the Western witchcraft phenomenon is Geoffrey Parrinder, an authority on comparative religion with anthropological persuasions. Parrinder regards the empirical claims of the belief as false and its consequences as brutal and regrettable. Nevertheless in order to understand why it occurs one must appreciate its 'social character' – one must identify the social needs (or 'dis-eases', as he puts it) that the belief helps to satisfy.

The social conditions he identifies are such things as 'the disorders of European wars, the epidemics, the high child mortality, [and] the general unsettlement of religion and society'. On the societal level he can therefore describe witches as 'veritable martyrs to the easing of social conscience', and claim that: 'Society suffers from neuroses as do individuals. To clear itself from guilt society looks about for scapegoats on which to lay its faults.' (1970: 202) The social institution primarily responsible for the editing, synthesizing and development of the popular superstitions that eventually formed the theoretical basis for the phenomenon was the Christian Church. The social changes primarily responsible for its popular demise were better conditions and 'the enlightenment brought by modern education and a reformed religion'. (1970: 115)

On the personal or individual level Parrinder looks to modern psychology, particularly to explain voluntary confessions. He therefore makes reference to delusions, 'depressed personalities' and 'compulsion neurotics'.

All of this seems to be fairly straightforward analysis of the type one might expect from a social anthropologist with strong psychological persuasions. What is not so straightforward, and seems to be an unnecessary theoretical imposition upon the *European* situation, is Parrinder's borrowing of the model of the witch developed by Evans-Pritchard in his analysis of the *African* Azande.

> People have included witchcraft under the same heading as magic. But the two are essentially distinct, and no progress can be made in understanding

90

what witchcraft is about until the consideration of magic in the same category
is abandoned.   (Parrinder 1970:14)

To expand a bit upon what was said in the first chapter, according to Evans-
Pritchard the powers of the Zande 'witch' are purely psychic (non-
physical). To do witchcraft they have no need of charms, spells,
incantations, or any other magical devices.

Even if this is representative of the Azande, one wonders what leads
Parrinder to insist that it is also true of the Western witchcraft phenomenon,
to a point where he complains that:

> The confusion between witchcraft and sorcery runs right through the early
> [European] references . . . For many centuries there was no clear *distinction*,
> and even later on when some sort of *definition* of witchcraft had been arrived
> at the witch was liable to be accused of offenses which were properly
> magical.[2]   (Parrinder 1970: 18)

Why must it be that the Europeans were confused? Why could it not be that
their own definitions of or distinction between 'witch' and 'sorcerer' were
simply different? Why must what is African be true of what is European,
and the reverse? Our old friend, the theoretical universal, seems to be re-
emerging. We shall eventually argue that an unwarranted and widespread
intellectual predisposition to the universality of the witchcraft pheonomenon
is responsible. But this must wait upon the next stage of our analysis, the
witchcraft phenomenon in Africa.

We have first to reconsider the three analyses of the phenomenon in the
West in an effort to determine whether any clear model of it or of the witch
personality has emerged. Upon how much do our three experts agree and
upon how much do they differ?

The results are disappointing on both counts. Given the reality the
Christian 'literalists' assign to evil as a force in the world, the three analysts
do not even agree that witchcraft is an objective impossibility. When it
comes to identifying the 'essence' of witchcraft power, Summers has
recourse to Satan (evil), Thomas to an 'occult' intimately involved with
magic, and Parrinder to a *purely* psychical ability that is by definition *non-*
magical. All do certainly agree that the existence of witchcraft is indicative
of some unsettled social conditions. But when it comes to being more
precise about what these conditions are, the detailed (social) analyses differ
so much and become so relative to a particular historical period of Western
culture that one has reason to doubt their potential to give rise to any
generalized model of the witchcraft phenomenon.

---

[2]Our italics.

91

When it comes to the analysis of the witchcraft personality, the situation is more complex. All do agree about the existence of a *popular* stereotype of the malevolent witch – anti-social, malicious, deliberate, and secretive. But when it comes to the analysis *of* this popular stereotype, our experts once more disagree. Summers tends to support it (converting 'malevolent' into 'evil'). Thomas dismisses the stereotype as the product of a particular class out to legitimize its own interests, and portrays witchcraft as a rational protest against social oppression. Parrinder effectively treats witches, as individuals, as the innocent and unfortunate victims of social problems (involuntary confessions), or as psychologically disoriented personalities (voluntary confessions).

When it comes to the person who is *voluntarily* and *deliberately* a witch, one is led to question any basis for consensus. In addition to genuine intellectual disagreements, it appears that different methodological approaches lead to radically different causal analyses of the same phenomenon. Consequently as of today experts upon Western witchcraft have yet to evolve any commonly accepted model of it as a social phenomenon or of the witch as a personality-type.

3. Analyses of African Witchcraft

African peoples present some of the clearest examples of belief in witchcraft today . . . Geoffrey Parrinder (1970: 13)

As any kind of significant social movement, the Western witchcraft phenomenon is attributed to a primitive past. But one way in which it can be still better understood, according to social anthropologists and others, is to study contemporary manifestations of the witchcraft phenomenon in modern, 'primitive'[3] African societies. To Parrinder it is clear that European and African witchcraft share a great deal in common. This is the reason for his insistence that the Zande distinction between *psychical* witchcraft and *magical* sorcery must also hold for the West.

It follows, then, that Parrinder must argue that this same distinction is characteristic of African witchcraft generally, which he does. 'It is the considered opinion of the great majority of European scholars who have studied African witchcraft at first hand.' (1970: 14)

However, another social anthropologist and contemporary of Parrinder, Lucy Mair, has produced yet another analysis of the witchcraft phenomenon in which she pointedly rejects the relevance of this Zande distinction (or Evans-Pritchard's basic model) to witchcraft in Africa *generally*.

---

[3]For this rather curious juxtaposition of terms see Thomas 1973: 609.

Although Evans-Pritchard did not offer the Zande ideas about witchcraft as a model to which other peoples should be expected to conform, many later anthropologists have leant heavily on the distinction between witchcraft and sorcery . . . and have sought to distinguish witches from sorcerers by [the Zande] . . . criteria. They have met the nemesis of over-definition . . .[4]
(Mair 1969: 21)

Given their beliefs about the powers and behaviour of witches, Zande society is 'exceptional' when compared with other African societies. Mair agrees with Evans-Pritchard that witchcraft is essentially a mystical power, but in Zande society such power is exercised *in*voluntarily. In Africa generally, what Mair believes distinguishes witches, above all, is the deliberate, excessive, and unjustifiable destruction they wreak. For her, therefore, the basic, essential condition of either the deliberately malevolent witch or sorcerer is that they have an 'evil disposition':

Witchraft . . . is unambiguously evil. It may well be motivated. . . . But it is always held to be unjustified; the witch may have good cause for anger, but if he had not had an evil disposition he would not have expressed his anger in this way. (Mair 1969: 15–16)

We shall eventually question the hypothesis that African 'witchcraft' may be used to understand and explain Western witchcraft. At the moment we only go so far as to point out that, after initially finding that they agree that the historical evidence is insufficient to arrive at a satisfactory model of the Western witchcraft phenomenon, one is struck by this basic disagreement between Parrinder and Mair in their efforts to do the same for its contemporary African counterpart.

Parrinder goes on to outline those beliefs about witchcraft powers and behaviour that he finds to be most representative of Africa generally:

1. Witches are female. Very occasionally one may find a man accused of witchcraft, but in such cases it is likely that Africans have themselves become confused about the distinction between the psychical and the magical. The 'male witch' is best regarded as a wizard, magician, or sorcerer – someone who uses *magic* for malevolent purposes.

2. Such women meet in secret assemblies, at night. When travelling to these assemblies they take on the form of an animal and leave their physical bodies behind.

---

[4]'This distinction [between witchcraft and sorcery] arose out of the study of Azande [sic] witchcraft, but it has been applied to other contexts, even though its relevance to other African societies is nowadays much disputed.' (Thomas 1973: 551)

3. Witches prey upon non-witches who are neither deserving of nor responsible for the misfortunes they suffer.

4. Often the witch is thought to 'consume' the body or spirit of its victim in some psychical and/or physical fashion. The physical symptoms of this in the victim are disease or any wasting, lingering illness.

5. Witches are sometimes thought to derive certain of their powers from a 'witchcraft substance', either internal to the body of the witch, or kept by her in some external, secret place.

The witch-doctor is the enemy of the witch and of witchcraft generally. He 'must be an upright man, keeping his hands clean from evil, and wielding his great power solely in the interests of health and the welfare of society.' (Parrinder 1970: 183) He is the person the victim can go to for help – to cure his illness and to identify and disarm or destroy the witch who is tormenting him.

Though he is not a witch, following the adage that 'it takes one to know one', Parrinder is compelled to say that: 'He has to be *like* witches so that he may overcome them.'[5] By this he seems to mean that the witch-doctor has a certain potential that makes him akin to witches. But it is a potential, an affinity, that must be rigorously controlled. For if he were to realize this potential – to use it to serve his own malevolent ends – he himself will also become a witch. Since witch-doctors (as opposed to witches) are not supposed to serve malevolent ends, and since they often use medicines or magic to help the victims of witchcraft to identify, drive off, or to destroy witches, they are best classified as 'good' magicians or wizards.

Since Evans-Pritchard's seminal work, scholars have appreciated the value of setting witchcraft in its social context. It is then possible to identify and to assess the rational ends it serves, even if ultimately it is still a false belief.

For Mair the most important function of the witchcraft belief is to provide a causal and moral explanation for unmerited suffering and misfortune. The witch, with her evil disposition and mystical powers, remains steadfastly in the background, available to either the individual or the witch-doctor who needs to account for personal injustice.

Parrinder's appreciation of its rationality rests, once again, upon his identifying the social dis-eases of which it is a product and which it helps to contain. Given that witches are usually women and that witch-doctors are usually men, this would seem to indicate one dis-ease – a strong sexual

---

[5] Our italics.

antagonism between the two. Witchcraft may therefore be regarded as an effective measure to keep women subservient in African society.

The fact that witchcraft accusations are usually made against members of one's own (extended) family is indicative of a significant degree of what Parrinder terms 'kinship stress', a second dis-ease of contemporary African societies.

> This shows that the belief in witchcraft is not unreasonable, however mistaken it may be, for the sufferer may accuse people who he thinks have good reason to dislike him, or whom he himself distrusts.   (1970: 193)

A third dis-ease he sees is consequent to the stresses of modernity and development. African societies are undergoing rapid transformations – simultaneous social and industrial revolutions. Rapid changes increase personal anxieties; increased anxieties promote accident, failure, and ill-health. The appeal to witchcraft can be used to rationalize and to relieve any or all of these. The witch serves, once again, as the scapegoat for the neuroses of (African) society.

The contributions of psychology to the study of witchcraft in Africa are much greater than was the case in the West. The witchcraft phenomenon is alive, even said to be thriving, in many African societies. Detailed clinical studies are therefore possible.

On the social psychological level the tendency is to explain the phenomenon as a consequence of social 'stress' points, or neuroses, or dis-eases as Parrinder has put it. Here the tendency is to see the witch as a victim of social forces that are beyond her control, an involuntary scapegoat who is forced to confess to excesses that are patently empirically impossible, thereby highlighting in an indirect manner the underlying social problems for which the society must victimize her. In a reciprocal manner, having such people *to* blame helps societies to cope with and to control the underlying, hostile social forces.

If witchcraft in Africa is a manifestation of general social problems, then the way to combat it is with general social programmes that seek to get at its roots. This is why Parrinder recommends programmes of social engineering that will emphasize education ('enlightenment'), improved medical services, and religious beliefs that place greater emphasis upon spiritual values ('love') that are somehow antagonistic to the fearful atmosphere in which the witchcraft phenomenon thrives.

The person who is constrained to confess to witchcraft is one matter. What of the one who confesses to it voluntarily? The clinical term encountered most frequently is 'depressed personality', a form of personality disorder. This is a person whose problems cause them to become oppressed by so strong a sense of personal guilt that they one day, apparently spontaneously, 'confess' to 'crimes' that are morbidly excessive in nature.

The structure of the explanation of witchcraft in Africa closely parallels that of witchcraft in the West. On a conceptual level witchcraft provides an explanation for personal misfortune that is thought appropriate to a prescientific theoretical system. On the social level witchcraft is best regarded as an index of certain social stress points.

With reference to the analysis of the witch as an individual personality, the parallel pretty much continues. In general witches in Africa are women. (Scholars of Western witchcraft can only go so far as to say that most documented witchcraft accusations were made against women.) In both Africa and the West the witch personality stereotype is that of someone who is anti-social, deliberately, excessively and destructively malevolent and, to come to that personality characteristic with which we shall have some reason to be especially concerned, secretive.

When it comes to professional analyses and explanations of the witch personality, an immediate consideration is the patent empirical impossiblities of witch powers and crimes. It would therefore be said that witches who confess in a forced and involuntary manner are the innocent victims of social dis-eases. And since the stereotype in effect defines what a witch is, it is that to which they must be forced to confess. On the other hand, if someone confesses to witchcraft completely independently of any intimidation, it is explained by saying they have a disordered personality.

4. Using African Witchcraft to Understand Western Witchcraft

It may be too late now to recreate from historical records a detailed picture of a community in Europe where *the belief in witchcraft* was an active force . . . . To see the process of misfortune, suspicion, accusation and public reaction in its social setting . . . the enquirer must go to *a society where witchcraft is still taken for granted* . . . . This is still possible among the societies of simple technology which provide the main field of study of social anthropologists. Up to now this kind of study has been most actively pursued in Africa . . .[6]   (Mair 1969: 16–18)

The remnants of the Western witchcraft phenomenon are fragmentary and one-sided. The characteristics of the witch that remain derive from the popular stereotype[7] created by ecclesiastical and judicial authorities to

---

[6]Our italics.

[7]The work supposed to be done by [African] witches rests, as in late medieval Europe, upon the general ideas that people have as to the actions of witches, and upon the witches'

rationalize the persecution of human beings for impossible crimes. Consequently it is to this stereotype that Parrinder must have recourse when he wants to describe the behaviour and powers of the witch according to Western society. His chapter and sub-chapter headings, accordingly, include: Nocturnal Gatherings; Covens and Sabbaths; Dreams and Wandering Souls; Night-Flying; Animal Familiars; Cannibalism; The Black Mass; The Devil; Incubi and Succubi; Witches' Marks; Pacts with the Devil, etc. His accounts of what witches 'did' are prefaced by an endless stream of 'were supposed to', 'were believed to', 'were said to', etc. Such a level of popular superstition and phantasy symbolism is not conducive to serious, in-depth analysis. The basis upon which the scholar can proceed to do sociological, social psychological or clinical psychological studies of the phenomenon is fragile and slight.

It is therefore with considerable relief that Parrinder and Mair speak of the accessibility of the contemporary witchcraft phenomenon in Africa. History does not deny them access to it. The common characteristics of the African witch that Parrinder detailed above[8] may correspond to an African popular stereotype of their behaviour. But the causal analyses by means of which he explains witchcraft as a consequence of certain social dis-eases, or of a basic personality disorder, are derived originally from African sources and then transferred to (or imposed upon) the European situation.[9] This is why, in his causal analyses of the phenomenon in African society he can be much more detailed (attributing it to 'sexual antagonism', 'kinship stresses', 'unnatural accusations', 'awkward people', and 'unsettled society') than when imaginatively transposing analogous conditions onto European society ('the disorders of European wars, the epidemics, the high child mortality, [and] the general unsettlement of religion and society').[10]

5. Universals and Cross-Cultural Analyses

There is no reason to *assume* that witchcraft in Africa *is* the same as *was* witchcraft in Europe, anymore than there was reason to *assume* that the *English-language* concept 'witchcraft' may serve as an accurate translation of

---

confessions themselves.' (Parrinder 1970: 141) One may argue that such confessions also contribute to our image of the witch. We would suggest that confessions, involuntary or voluntary, are socially acceptable only if they conform to the stereotype. In other words, one is a witch only if one confesses to certain types of crimes, as prescribed by the stereotype.
[8] See pp.93–94.
[9] Compare with Thomas: 'there is in principle no reason why the social context of witchcraft accusations should have been the same in different societies.' (1973: 677)
[10] See p.90 above.

its supposed *African-language* equivalents. Whatever is translated as being 'witchcraft' in Africa (or even in one place in Africa) *may* well be a very different thing from whatever is elsewhere in the world and history. The introduction of a broad universal may make for more fruitful cross-cultural analyses and comparisons, but the arguments justifying its introduction must be carefully assessed.

In this section we begin by examining the relations between three propositions which have been defended by some or all of the authorities whose theories we have considered. It appears that the three may not be entirely consistent:

(1) There is insufficient historical data remaining to arrive at any accurate understanding or explanation of Western witchcraft.

(2) Witchcraft in Africa today can be used to understand and to explain what witchcraft in the West once was.

(3) Witchcraft in Africa today closely resembles what witchcraft in the West once was.

There would appear to be some inconsistency in maintaining that one does not understand one phenomenon (Western witchcraft), and at the same time maintaining that that phenomenon is effectively the same as another phenomenon (African 'witchcraft') that one can understand. One explanation for why this can be done is that there is a tacit assumption about the universality of witchcraft. The 'two' may then be treated as different *manifestations* of the *same phenomenon*.

Certainly that is the implication of the quotation from Mair above (p.96). If historical contingencies make it impossible to study Western witchcraft, the investigator is advised to pack his bags and depart for Africa. Parrinder is careful to reserve judgement on whether African and Western witchcraft (causally) derive from a common historical antecedent. Nevertheless he finds the similarities between them so striking that they effectively become equivalent:

> ... the study of witchcraft is not merely antiquarian, made up of guesses about the mentality of medieval Europeans, but it is one whose interpretation can be greatly eased by a consideration of practices believed in by millions of people today.   (1970: 128)
>
> ... some of the [witchcraft] ideas have a family likeness because they are of almost universal occurrence ... in the interpretation of witchcraft today European and African beliefs are often cited together.   (1970: 15)
>
> Although beliefs comparable with those of European witchcraft have been known in many parts of the world, it is in Africa that the most careful and extensive study has been made of them.   (1970: 128)

> To the subject of witchcraft I have given five years' intensive study and much
> longer general interest during twenty years in Africa.   (1970: 10)

In the above quotations Parrinder intimates more than the equivalence of Western and African witchcraft. He comes close to maintaining the basic identity of the phenomenon in any historical period anywhere in the world.

With what sort of evidence does he support this claim to universality? Parrinder differs from Thomas and Mair when, in assessing the state of scholarship with reference to Western witchcraft, he says such things as: 'the records of the witch trials are *wonderfully comprehensive*'[11] (1970: 11) and, 'This has led to a scrutiny of much of the literature of both African and European beliefs in witchcraft, because they are now *so well documented*'.[12] (1970: 16) Compare these evaluative statements with Thomas's own: 'the survival of legal records has been *so patchy* as to provide an *uncertain basis for generalization*.'[13] (1973: 535)

Even Parrinder admits that:

> Our knowledge of European witchcraft is almost entirely derived from the writings of the persecutors, or from the records of confessions said to have been given by or extorted from the people accused of witchcraft. (1970: 103)

The bias inherent in such sources is implicitly acknowledged, but Parrinder believes that it can be controlled by correcting, supplementing, or even substantiating it with the understanding gained from the study of witchcraft in Africa. Again we question whether he is entitled to reach this conclusion. His assertion that the records are 'wonderfully comprehensive' is disputed by Thomas and Mair. Paradoxically even Parrinder acknowledges the bias[14] of these same records, and then proceeds to claim that they can be used to prove that witchcraft in the West was essentially the same as it is in Africa.

The evidential basis for this final inference is not clear. It is the *lack* of evidence (and the consequent *lack* of understanding) about Western witchcraft that leads the scholar to turn to its African counterpart. But he is only entitled to use African witchcraft in this way if he can be assured that it is an equivalent. And he is only entitled to treat it as an equivalent if the existing evidence is sufficient to prove that it is.

If this representation of the argument is fair, it is a rather clear example of circular reasoning, or of *petitio principii* (begging the question). One

---

[11-13]Our italics.

[14]A bias which Thomas uses to argue for their not being representative of what was in fact happening. See p. 89 above.

assumes what one needs to prove (that the two are equivalent) in order to prove what one wants to prove (that African 'witchcraft' can be used to understand and explain Western witchcraft). However, we would go one step further and suggest that a further hidden assumption, or intellectual predisposition, leads to this fallacy's being regarded as a perfectly legitimate inference: the presumption that the witchcraft phenomenon is a cultural universal and that therefore whatever it is today in Africa must be representative of whatever it once was in the West. This presumption is particularly blatant in the Mair quotation on page 96 above. She begins with the assumption that witchcraft is a universal. The only thing to decide is in which society one is going to study it.

We said earlier on that one of the aims of this chapter was to see of what use Western models of witchcraft and of the witch personality could be in understanding and explaining the behaviour of people in non-Western societies in the first place[15]. Western scholars were left with a rather superficial stereotype that provided an unsatisfactory basis for serious analysis.

This was the ecclesiastical and judicial stereotype to which Thomas made reference. It had two facets. The first was an elaborate, primarily theological superstructure expressed in extremely technical language that explained how witches came by their powers and how they could be controlled or destroyed. No doubt some members of the upper classes took this facet of the stereotype seriously. However Thomas suggests that it also provided a rationalization for the intimidation and disciplining of the poor. These theories attributed much of the misery of the lower classes to the acts of members *of* the lower classes. The underprivileged were thereby encouraged to turn against one another rather than against those with vested interests in the existent social and economic system.

The real possibility that these theories were in significant measure rationalizations promoted by those with vested interests, coupled with a growing scepticism about the reality of the (evil) spiritual roots of Western witchcraft, has led to the distrust of and even disinterest in them. The occasional reference to the dusty tomes in which these theories and formulae were collected occurs in contemporary horror films. But, locked away in equally dusty libraries and deliberately made unavailable to the general public, they no longer exercise a significant influence upon Western intellectual thought.

---

[15] With the exception of the Christian literalist approach, and of historically and geographically limited studies like Thomas's in which the interest in or the claims to the cultural universality of witchcraft are insignificant.

The second facet to this stereotype was the de-intellectualized form in which it was communicated to the lower classes.[16] Whatever remains of the 'popular' stereotype of the witch in Western society today derives mainly from the remnants of this facet. This would include most of what we refer to as the 'fantasy symbolism' associated with witchcraft in the West.

How much of an improvement upon this dated, fragmentary and parochial stereotype are the analyses of Parrinder and Mair? This is a question to which no final answer may be arrived at until we have attempted our own analysis of what has been treated as the witchcraft phenomenon in Yoruba society. For the moment we shall only make the following observations. We question the adequacy of Parrinder's defence of the Zande distinction between witchcraft and magic as being the most fundamental and universal criterion for understanding witchcraft anywhere in the world. We do not question the erudition and sensitivity underlying Evans-Pritchard's research. But we will question Parrinder's insistence that the Zande model be taken as archetypal of both African and European witchcraft, to a point where he describes any African or European witch or scholar of witchcraft who disagrees with it as confused.

Mair's alternative, the evil disposition, is also open to question. Because of its close association with Christian eschatology, on a connotative basis if nothing else, 'evil' is an inappropriate concept to use as a cultural universal. It suggests that the traditional Christian dichotomy of a (physical *and* spiritual) world divided up between the forces of light and darkness may be taken as a model for any conceptual system in which something akin to witchcraft occurs.

From our earlier discussions of Quine we are familiar with the problems and dangers inherent in cross-cultural comparisons. Our aim is not to exaggerate those problems to a point where any proposed cross-cultural model for witchcraft becomes hopelessly biased by the language and beliefs of the culture in which it originates. We propose now to undertake the analysis of the presumed theoretical equivalent to 'witchcraft' in the Yoruba conceptual system. On the basis of this analysis we shall then suggest that the models developed by both Parrinder and Mair are incomplete because they are, effectively, based upon a popular *African* stereotype of what the witch must be. We believe that we have found a way to penetrate beyond this stereotype that will allow us to understand better what the Yoruba 'witches' in fact believe they are.

---

[16] It should also be noted that elements of this facet diverged from the 'official' version put out by the higher authorities, as with the insistence on the part of the lower classes upon a distinction between good and bad witches.

6. The Àjẹ́ *in Yoruba Society*

(1) *Àjẹ́* are just like thieves, because no one who is a thief would tell others that he was. So also *àjẹ́* will not reveal their identity to any person.

A person who is anti-social and deliberately and destructively malevolent towards other members of his community has to keep such feelings and the actions motivated by them secret. Otherwise the community would turn against and, if necessary, destroy him.

As we have said, *àjẹ́* is the Yoruba word most commonly translated into English as 'witch'. Both Parrinder (who spent most of his twenty years in Africa studying the Yoruba) and Mair assert that the Yoruba beliefs about, attitudes towards and definitions of *àjẹ́* closely match the models for African witchcraft that they have devised.

Indeed there is a certain popular image of the *àjẹ́* that does contain many of the behavioural characteristics of the African witch that they have previously noted. Compare the following statements made by Yoruba *onísẹ̀gùn* with Parrinder's list on pp.93–94 above:

(2) *1.* But when we say that an *àjẹ́* is 'confessing' [i.e. admitting to their crimes after an *onísẹ̀gùn* has made them take medicine meant to curtail their powers] – those who confess are usually women.

(3) *2.* The *àjẹ́* have an *ẹgbẹ́* (society), and also a place where they meet.

(4) The *àjẹ́* does not cry out in the afternoon. All these are the work of the night.

(5) When we sleep *àjẹ́* can turn into spirit [form] and harm other *èniyàn* (persons).

(6) They can change into any type of animal . . .

(7) *Àjẹ́* can turn into a snake and bite a person. *Àjẹ́* can turn into a dry tree [e.g. a dead branch] which will fall on a person and kill him.

(8) *3.* The *àjẹ́* behaves badly to other persons without any cause at all, while the ordinary *èniyàn* (person) will have a reason for their behaviour.

(9) *Àjẹ́* is the one which is thought capable of the worst kind of thing.

(10) *4.* There are *àjẹ́* who will kill their children, but will pretend and cry when the child dies. Whereas it is the cause of death.

(11) *5.* They have certain things inside them which are similar to birds. These they use to do various kinds of extraordinary things. There are many types of *àjẹ́*. Some have their own [*àjẹ́* substance] in the eyes. Some in the head. Some in the stomach. Some inside the soil. And some have theirs in basins and put them on the table. These kind [the last] don't take human blood – only animal blood. But they can control it [the substance in the basin] and use it for many things.

If the behavioural sketch constituted by the above quotations is representative of the meaning of *àjẹ́* in Yoruba culture, Parrinder's model would appear to be strongly confirmed. And quotation 8 comes close to a behavioural equivalent of Mair's evil disposition.

We will argue that the quotations are indeed representative, but only of a kind of Yoruba popular stereotype that is analogous to the one that may be (re)constructed out of remnants of European fantasy symbolism (pacts with the Devil, cannibalism, night-flying, etc.) We begin by drawing attention to a particular manifestation of the *àjẹ́* phenomenon that seems to have been previously unreported or ignored. It also appears to be that manifestation of the phenomenon that the *oníṣẹ̀gùn* are most reticent to discuss, probably because it involves them in a most immediate and intimate manner. But once the barrier of secrecy has been breached, even if in a circuitous way, the role of the *àjẹ́* in Yoruba society and personality theory becomes more clear.

The problem first introduced itself over the issue of the ratio of female to male *àjẹ́* in Yoruba society. Although quotation 2 affirms that most public *confessions* to being *àjẹ́* are made by women, when asked about the relative ratio of men to women who actually *are àjẹ́*, the *oníṣẹ̀gùn* said:

> (12) The same. There may be many among men. But while men will stop thinking of something, the eyes of women will still be there [i.e. the male *àjẹ́* are more successful at concealing themselves].

Or when asked whether it was the case that more women than men were *àjẹ́*:

> (13) This is not true. For example, [it may be that] we call *àjẹ́* 'the mother of children' (*iyá àwọn ọmọdé*). We do not say 'the father of children' because this is not how we refer [idiomatically] to the *àjẹ́*.

Our concern became to identify who and where the male *àjẹ́* were. They were said to be as or even more powerful than the women, but apparently were much more adept at concealing themselves.

Let us go back over some of the history of our relationship with the *oníṣẹ̀gùn*. As was noted in the Introduction, we work with them on an individual basis. We are forbidden to disclose the information we obtain from one to any of the others. However in 1975 one felt mandated to make a statement (Hallen 1996: 220–221), on his own behalf and on that of the others, explaining a vital element of their methodology. Part of this statement amounted to the following: it is primarily the intelligence, ability and talent of the individual *oníṣẹ̀gùn* that is responsible for the power and success of his prescriptions and treatment. When dealing with the general public and the individual patient, he may attribute his success primarily to the power of the supreme deity or to one of the lesser divinities. But this is a deception to which the *onísègùn* must have recourse. *For if he were to claim the responsibility for himself, he would risk being identified by other members of the community as* àjẹ́, *and this could lead to his personal and professional ruin.*

At first glance this makes it sound as if any *onísègùn* (and perhaps by extension any other 'professional' person) who has the talent and ability to be exceptionally good at his trade and therefore very successful at it, *and* the audacity to proclaim this in any obviously public manner, runs the risk of being identified as *àjẹ́* by other members of the community. And, indeed, in the witchcraft literature reference is occasionally made to this secondary function of the witchcraft phenomenon, of its being a device to keep the unusually talented in their place:

> In a primitive society, witch-beliefs of this kind can act as a severe check to technical progress by discouraging efficiency and innovation. A man who gets ahead in a tribal society is likely to awaken the suspicions of his neighbours. Among the Bemba of Northern Rhodesia, for example, it is said that to find a beehive with honey in the woods is good luck; to find two beehives is very good luck; to find three is witchcraft. In such an environment, witch-beliefs help to sustain a rough egalitarianism. They are a conservative force, acting as a check upon undue individual effort.   (Thomas 1973:643)

Certainly any number of statements made by the *onísègùn* seem to support this interpretation:

> (14) In addition, he [the *onísègùn*] may even know medicine to the point that people may want to run from him. They will say he is *àjẹ́* . . .

> (15) The word of mouth can make one person to be regarded as *àjẹ́*. There are some people who will say something and it will be like that. When he says so, it will happen like that. And you can call this kind of person any kind of name.

> (16) If someone is more brilliant than his mates, we may refer to him as *àjẹ́* . . .

> (17) There is one which could be regarded as *àjẹ́*. For example, if you are doing something which is always right without anyone telling you [what to do] . . .

> (18) They call that kind of person *àjẹ́* because he always says the truth. His words never miss. They will say that if his dreams are always coming to be true, people will say he has already finished everything by the night.

Is this where the case is to rest, then? That the Yoruba stereotype can be said to conform so closely to the European one because it is indicative of parallel social dis-eases, and on a secondary level the appellation '*àjẹ́*' can be seen as a device for controlling the exceptionally talented person so that he dare not disturb the 'closed' equilibrium of traditional society?

We cannot agree with this. Moreover, we have found that the *onísẹ̀gùn* do not either, and this is the missing yet vital element to a complete understanding of *àjẹ́*. For a point that is also apparent from quotations 14–18 above is the repeated references to 'they will say', 'you can call', 'we may refer', 'they call that kind of person', and so forth. With this rhetoric the *onísẹ̀gùn* are making reference to what the ordinary person takes to be behavioural characteristics associated with the *àjẹ́*. But a further dimension to the significance of these characteristics was suggested by other remarks, also made by the *onísẹ̀gùn* but in a more personal manner, such as the following:

> (19) There are some people, called *àjẹ́*, who are supernatural. But whenever they do any supernatural thing, if you were to ask them how it is possible for them to do such a thing, they would attribute it to the power of *Ọlọ́run* [the supreme deity]. *Ọlọ́run* is just like something under which persons hide to apply all our powers. *Ọlọ́run* stands as a shield under which everyone hides to apply whatever power he possesses.

What this eventually suggested to us was that the gentleman concerned might be trying to intimate that many of the *onísẹ̀gùn* are *àjẹ́*. In other words, that the above preceding quotations can also be interpreted so as to suggest that the reason a person becomes one of the most powerful and successful of the *onísẹ̀gùn* is because of his own special abilities, and those abilities may derive from the fact that he has the *àjẹ́*.

Would this then require that such *onísẹ̀gùn* must be regarded as antisocial and malevolent? For that should be a consequence if Parrinder's or Mair's models apply. We are convinced that the answer to this question is negative, but before we can introduce supporting statements by the *onísẹ̀gùn* it will first be necessary to provide brief explanations of a number of supplementary Yoruba concepts that will also eventually prove to be critical building blocks of our theory of Yoruba personality-types.

For the Yoruba the essential elements of the person (*èniyàn*) when in the world are the body (*ara*), the vital spirit of that body, or soul (*ẹ̀mí*), and the destiny (*orí*) that will determine every significant event during that particular lifetime. The concept of '*orí*' is an exceedingly complex and fascinating one, and a good deal of literature already exists on the subject. But all we need say of it here is that the same spirit (*ẹ̀mí*) returns to the world an indefinite number of times, each time with a new destiny (*orí*) which it consciously, deliberately and *freely* chooses before being reborn.

Therefore, when the *onísẹ̀gùn* make a remark such as the following:

> (20) The *àjẹ́* behaves according to how its *ẹ̀mí* is. Not all of them do bad things.

what they also have in mind is that even after death, when existing only as *èmí*, the person is still a *moral* being with a character (*ìwà*) that may be assessed as good or bad. And it is this moral element that plays a significant role in influencing the kind of destiny (*orí*) the person will choose for his next lifetime. If he is a good person (*ènìyàn rere*), he will choose a destiny that will entail his doing good things while in the world. If he is a bad person (*ènìyàn burúkú*), he will choose one that entails the opposite, though he will see it as being to his benefit. This interpretation of Yoruba beliefs about life and afterlife is in part supported by the following statements:

(21) The *ìwà* of *àjẹ́* . . . there are some *àjẹ́* whose *ìwà* is good.

(22) It is inside your *ìwà* [character] that you bring out *ènìyàn rere*. If he is a *babaláwo*[17] and you bring a child to him [because it has some problem], if there are some people who are trying to be cruel to the child, he will drive them away. He will not allow them to come. As a *babaláwo* all his medicine will be answering (*jé*) [i.e. be effective]. If there is any *àjẹ́* who is going to disturb him, he will drive him away. He is *àjẹ́ rere*, *àlùjànún rere* and *ènìyàn rere*. He will combine everything. If he is not a *babaláwo*, but if a babaláwo is making his medicine, he will not allow them [*ènìyàn burúkú*] to spoil it, and he will tell the *babaláwo* to change his hand [i.e. how to improve his techniques so that they will not be fallible]. He will teach him. This is good *àlùjànún*.

We will undertake some explanation of the difficult term '*àlùjànún*' a bit later on.[18] For the moment our interest centers on the expression '*àjẹ́ rere*', good *àjẹ́*, in quotation 22 and its implied equivalent in quotation 20. Is it being used here in a metaphorical sense, as an expressive way of referring to an exceptionally talented individual? Or does it mean that there really can be *àjẹ́* who are neither malevolent nor anti-social, who in fact work for the positive betterment of mankind? The answer to this question may be obtained from the following:

(23) There are some who behave well, if they have chosen to be so from heaven. This type of *àjẹ́* will not associate themselves with others [*àjẹ́*] who are known to be bad.

(24) *Àjẹ́* is *ènìyàn rere*. Not all the *àjẹ́* are *ènìyàn burúkú*. There are some good ones.

(25) *Àjẹ́ rere* cannot do anything bad. He will be looking for good things. And he will not be eating blood.

And finally, a remark made in discussion with specific reference to the issue of whether it is possible for a *babaláwo/oníṣẹ̀gùn* to be *àjé*, *àlùjànún*, and *ènìyàn rere* (a good person) at the same time:

---

[17]For the meaning of this term see p.1 above. However, when referring to themselves in discussion, the *oníṣẹ̀gùn* often use the terms '*oníṣẹ̀gùn*' and '*babaláwo*' interchangeably.
[18]See p.107.

(26) I said it was possible. The *babaláwo* who has *àlùjànún* and *àjẹ́*, their medicine will always answer (*je*) [i.e. work well]. He should have seen the *idí*[19] of what he wants to use the medicine for . . . As *àjé* and *àlùjànún*, any medicine which I put my hands on must be good.

The answer to our original question, then, is that there definitely are many *àjẹ́* who are *good* persons; furthermore, that some of them are *onísègùn* or *babaláwo*, in fact the most powerful amongst the *onísègùn* or *babaláwo*. And since the gentlemen with whom we are holding our discussions are considered to be amongst the most powerful of the *onísègùn* in the area, the implication is definite and clear. Many amongst them are knowingly *àjẹ́*. But they dare not admit to it in an open and direct manner. The closest they can come is to state it in the hypothetical manner found in the final sentence of quotation 26.

We have yet finally to conclude why this reluctance to admit to being *àjẹ́*, why the need for secrecy, exist. But before we get to this we must first say something about the concept of '*àlùjànún*':

(27) If you come to ask something from me now, I can tell you to go and come back. I will put that thing in mind (*okòn*[20]). And when I see (*ríran*) it, if it is something that will not be possible, I will say so. If it is good, I will tell you to go there – that there is nothing [no problem]. It means that I've used the *ojú inú* (literally: 'inside' eye) to see (*wo*) it.

As is the case with *àjẹ́*, *àlùjànún* confers a certain power upon a person. In the above example, the closest English-language equivalent is perhaps 'second sight', a kind of telepathic power (the 'inside' eye) that allows a person to foresee the consequences of an action. People who are *àlùjànún* are therefore considered among the most powerful in Yoruba society.

7. Is the Àjẹ́ a Witch?

If one goes by the criteria, or model(s), of African witchcraft drawn up by Parrinder and Mair, the *àjẹ́* appear not to fit them in at least four important respects:

1. Many *àjẹ́* are men.

2. Many *onísègùn* are *àjẹ́*. According to Parrinder's model the *onísègùn* are one important professional group in Yoruba society who would be classed under the anachronistic heading of 'witch-doctor'. A person who is being troubled by *àjẹ́* will often go to an *onísègùn* for help with identifying the *àjẹ́*,

See p.70 above. '*idí*' is a component of '*nwádi*' and a noun form of 'bottom', 'cause' or reason'.

For the meaning of this term see p.61 above.

and for counsel and medicine to counter their onslaught. But it is Parrinder who insists that the witch-doctor can*not* be a witch.[21]

3. Many *àjẹ́* use medicine to achieve their ends. Granted sometimes it may be because they are *oníṣẹ̀gùn*, rather than that they are *àjẹ́*, that is the primary reason for their practising medicine. But it is clear that there are *àjẹ́* who are *neither oníṣẹ̀gùn nor babaláwo*[22] and still make use of medicine to achieve their ends:

> (28) If the *àjẹ́* learns the medicine for making rain, it will fall immediately. And if he wants to take [prevent] it, he will do this easily. They can do both easily.
>
> (29) This can be done by means of medicine, especially if he is *àjẹ́* . . . he could use a medicine which would make it impossible for the leopard to see him. . . . These are the works of medicine.
>
> (30) Persons, like *àjẹ́*, . . . are those who are responsible . . . If the 'powerfuls' want to travel to somewhere like Lagos, they will be making a lot of preparation [i.e. medicine] in the afternoon. And when it is night time, they will tie all the medicine on their body. Then they will rise from the earth to the sky and they will be moving . . .

Parrinder has stated categorically that witchcraft must not be confused with sorcery. Witchcraft is a *purely* psychical phenomenon, and one who makes the mistake of associating it with the preparation or use of 'magical' medicines is confusing the sorcerer, the good magician, the witch-doctor, or the wizard, with witchcraft proper. But, as the above quotations indicate, the Yoruba are either confused (a possibility we shall discuss in the final sub-section of this chapter) or attribute properties to the *àjẹ́* which do not suit Parrinder's model.

If the *àjẹ́* do make use of 'magical' medicines, is this the source of their power? And if it is not medicine, what is? These are extremely difficult questions to answer, and have been from the very beginning. Thomas may attribute it to the occult, Parrinder to psychical power, and Mair to a mystical ability, but what precisely are these terms meant to convey other than that the basis for the power of witchcraft exceeds the boundaries of ordinary or scientific understanding and explanation. Witchcraft is *extra-*ordinary. Witchcraft is *super*-natural.

Is it the same with the Yoruba *àjẹ́*? This is a question to which we can only give a partial and somewhat speculative answer, though to attempt even this we must first introduce a few more technical terms from the Yoruba conceptual system.

---

[21]See p.94 above.

[22]That there are *àjẹ́* who are neither *oníṣẹ̀gùn* nor *babaláwo* is also indicated by the last three sentences of quotation 22 above.

First, let us go back to the question of how a person first becomes *àjẹ́*. We have already made reference to the way *ẹ̀mí* chooses its destiny (*orí*) before coming to the world (i.e. being born), but let us now go over it a bit more carefully:

(31) They [the *àjẹ́*] are *ènìyàn* (persons), just like you and me.

(32) You cannot use medicine to make *àjẹ́*.

(33) This is what they [*àjẹ́*] brought from heaven.

(34) *Ọlọ́run* (the supreme deity) puts the *àṣẹ* on their destiny (*orí*).

(35) There are some *ènìyàn* (persons) who are only *àjẹ́* and not the others [i.e. *àlùjànún*, etc.]. It depends upon the choice of individual.

When the individual (as *ẹ̀mí*) has chosen a new destiny (*orí*) he then appears before *Ọlọ́run*, the supreme deity, who uses his supreme power, the *àṣẹ*, to 'fix' that destiny to the individual so that it will guide and channel the person's approaching lifetime in the world. Assumption to the power of *àjẹ́*, then, is something that is said to happen to a person before they are born into the physical world.

Secondly, although being *àjẹ́* is said to be the function of choosing a particular *orí*, the choice *of* that *orí* has serious consequences for the *ẹ̀mí* or *inú* of the person who then comes into the world:

(36) There are some with two *ẹ̀mí*. *Àjẹ́* has two *ẹ̀mí*.

(37) *Àjẹ́* has two *inú*.

(38) They were born with them [people with two *inú*]. They do not simply come by them in the world. It is part of their destiny.

(39) In the most common use of the word (*nipata ki*) [the word referred to is *inú*], when we say that someone has got *inú* we mean that he is a good person (*omolúàbí*). In another way you can say that someone has got *inú* to mean that he has got [the power of] *àjẹ́*.

(40) It is his *ìwà* (character), because the *ìwà* is *inú*. All the things we do come out of *inú*.

(41) A person (*ènìyàn*) cannot have anything apart from the thing which is given to him in heaven . . . If the *inú* of someone is good, bad things will not have a place there. If we teach him to do bad things, he will not accept. Whenever a person is instigated to do bad things, if he agrees, this means that it is his own will.

Because of the peculiarities of their medicinal and theoretical systems, the *oníṣẹ̀gùn* have reason to be specially concerned with and interested in the *inú* of a person. *Inu* literally means 'inside'. It can also be used to refer to the stomach. But for purposes of our present exposition, rather than becoming involved with the intricacies of the medicinal system, it is sufficient to point out that *inú* and *ẹ̀mí* are also sometimes used by them interchangeably (as may be inferred from quotations 37–39 above).

What does a second *èmí* or *inú* enable the *àjẹ́* to do? This is perhaps the most difficult question of all to answer. As far as the stereotype is concerned, it certainly is the source of the powers of the *àjẹ́* when in the world.[23] And as a 'vital spirit', *èmí/inú* is certainly more or other than material substance. As a second vital element, it is this *àjẹ́ èmí/inú* that the person can send out or use to go out and away from himself to accomplish those things that make him extraordinary.

This (coupled with quotation 33 above) would apparently indicate that the source of the power of the *àjẹ́* is not medicine. But it would be an error to therefore conclude that the power of *àjẹ́* has nothing to do with medicine, including what Parrinder would refer to as 'magic'. If *àjẹ́* makes medicine it is thought to be more powerful and more effective *as* medicine than what would be prepared by a person with no special power or ability. The exact nature of the causal connection between the *àjẹ́* and the power of its medicines still eludes us,[24] but there is not doubt but that it is there.

One further, possibly minor but still interesting, point about the powers of the *àjẹ́* is brought out by several remarks in which the *oníṣẹ̀gùn* compare them with those of the *àlùjànún*:

(42) *Àjẹ́* cannot know what is going on in the next room, whereas *emèrè*[25] and *àlùjànún* can.

(43) *Emèrè* can detect what a person has done in secret, but *àjẹ́* cannot.

(44) If someone holds something in his [closed] hand, *emèrè* can identify what it is. But *àjẹ́* cannot.

'Paranormal perception', 'clairvoyance', 'telepathy' and even 'mind-reading' are all rather technical English-language terms in the field sometimes referred to as parapsychology. On a more prosaic level that will enable us to avoid becoming entangled with the various theories underlying this controversial field of interest, what the above quotations seem to indicate (when coupled with quotation 27) is that, while the *àlùjànún* can both 'send' (or 'transmit') and 'receive', the *àjẹ́* can only 'send'. This would mean that the power of the *àjẹ́* is demonstrated primarily by the ability to

---

[23]As recounted on p.102 above.

[24]Another reason for the problem of obtaining more specific information about this is the element of secrecy (*awo*) surrounding the making of medicines, in addition to that surrounding the powers of the *àjẹ́*. For further information about the role of secrecy in professional associations in Yoruba culture see Abimbola and Hallen 1993.

[25]Another apparent personality-type to which we shall make brief reference in the next sub-section. For the moment the important things are what the *àjẹ́* cannot do rather than what the *emèrè* can do.

use the second *ẹmí/inú* to do something for it, even if it is distant from the body with which it is associated. The *àlùjànún*, however, in some manner for future researchers to look into, is able to know about (to receive information about) events that are going on distant from him *as well as* to do something about them, if he so chooses.

4. Many *àjẹ́* are neither evil nor malevolent. In fact many *àjẹ́* may be characterized as benevolent and eminently moral persons. Numerous remarks of the *onísẹ̀gùn* support these assertions (quotations 22, 23–25, 41, 42), and therefore they do not seem to require any further defence. But it is important to recall that, for Mair, an evil disposition and, for Parrinder, deliberate malice were important, sometimes even essential, characteristics of the witch.

In this sub-section we have drawn attention to four important respects in which Yoruba beliefs about the *àjẹ́* differ from the models of African witchcraft formulated by Parrinder and Mair, and to which the Yoruba are said by them to subscribe. We would therefore suggest that their models are inadequate, or at least incomplete, for providing an adequate basis for analysis and understanding of the *àjẹ́* phenomenon in Yoruba thought.

What we would suggest as an alternative is a two-tiered model, or perhaps two models – one to suit the popular stereotype (for this Parrinder's and Mair's would be satisfactory), and a second comparatively esoteric model of the *àjẹ́* based upon the remarks of the *onísẹ̀gùn*. According to one the *àjẹ́* is an extremely dangerous and destructive anti-social personality that must be sought out and destroyed whenever possible. According to the other the *àjẹ́* may be used for the benefit, welfare, defence and development of mankind. We shall have occasion to speculate how these two conflicting models arose in the next sub-section of this chapter.

8. Àjé *as a Personality-Type*

(45) You know, people are different from each other and some have more power (*àṣẹ*) than others. Their *ẹmí* is different from others.

(46) The power of the *àjẹ́* is different ... This special power is given by *Ọlọ́run*.

In professional psychology basic personality types vary between different theories. Adler proposes the ruling, getting and avoiding types, and the good man. Freudian theory prefers the oral sucking, oral biting, anal sadistic and anal retentive. Fromm writes of receptive, exploitative, hoarding and productive characters. And Jung speaks of introverts and extroverts. Sometimes such types are defined in purely behavioural terms.

But personality theory (in professional psychology) also entertains a meaning of personality that:

> refers to the fundamental or basic core of man, to the essential person that lives at the centre of our being... Because of its innate properties, personality in this ... sense is usually seen as autonomous and unchanging: one's overt behaviour may vary from situation to situation, but the real causes of one's actions tend to remain constant. (Hogan 1976)

In the Western tradition witchcraft – being called 'witch' – referred to more than behaviour. It was meant to say something about the state of the person's insides, or soul, for lack of a better word. Consider the following definition, culled from the *Symbolaeographie* of William West, written in 1594 (Ewen 1971: 23):

> A witch or hagg[26] is she which being eluded[27] by a league[28] made with the deuil[29] through his perswasion, inspiration and iudling[30] thinketh she can designe what manner of euil things soeuer, either by thought or imprication[31]
> . . .

The dominant terms with reference to the witch personality are 'wicked' and 'evil'. By virtue of a pact with the supreme spiritual enemy of mankind, a human being has in effect become anti-human. It is this spiritual force of evil that has transformed the witch's soul and that is the source of the malevolence that prompts he or she to become the enemy of the innocent and good. The witch personality *is* evil.

When the *oníṣẹ̀gùn* speak of a person being *àjẹ́*, they generally do not use a form of the verb 'to be'. Consider the following:

(47) If I have *àjẹ́* ... during my sleep I can go into the bush ...

(48) In using the *àjẹ́* we don't combine our own to do things [*àjẹ́* seldom work together].

The *oníṣẹ̀gùn* do not say that a person *is àjẹ́*. They say he *has àjẹ́* or that he *uses àjẹ́*. Similarly, with reference to *àlùjànún:*

(49) If my *àlùjànún* is not enough ...

(50) We think he did all this with *àlùjànún.*

---

[26]'a witch; sometimes an infernally wicked woman' (*Shorter Oxford English Dictionary* 1965). [27]'befooled'. [28]'a covenant or compact made between parties for their mutual protection and assistance'. [29]'Devil: the supreme spirit of evil'.

[30]'Curers of diseases which for the curing of all sicknesses and sores of man and beast, vse eyther certeine superstitious words or writings called charmes or spelles hanged about the necke or some other part of the body' (Ewen 1971: 23).

[31]'the action of imprecating, or invoking evil upon any one, in an oath or adjuration; cursing' (*Shorter Oxford English Dictionary* 1965).

The phrasing here implies that the self, the *personal* self, is somehow distinct from whatever special abilities or powers a person may have. Why this is the case may perhaps be explained by yet again making reference to the process through which a person first becomes *àjẹ́*. For the *ẹ̀mí* evidently was a kind of consciousness, a kind of personality, at the moment it is choosing a new destiny (*orí*) before it comes into the world. It must, otherwise there would be no agent to undertake the choosing. And, as importantly, it has a *moral* character. A bad person (as *ẹ̀mí*) can therefore choose, quite deliberately, a life of malevolence, of inflicting miseries upon other people. Such a life need not require that the person have any special powers. The majority of people in the world do not. These are the ordinary persons. And it is perfectly possible for *ẹ̀mí* to choose a life that will allow him to be an ordinarily nasty or malevolent person. But the key determining element, as we have just said, is the moral character of the *ẹ̀mí* that does the choosing before coming into the world. This is what will determine, if it chooses to have *àjẹ́*, whether it will at the same time choose a life that will entail using the *àjẹ́* for the benefit rather than for the destruction of mankind.

Diagrammatically it would look something like this:

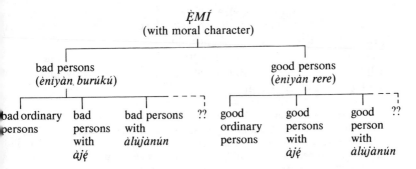

The question marks represent further special abilities or powers that have not been listed, such as the *emèrè* referred to in quotation 42 above. But the diagram is also incomplete in another equally important sense. It is possible for the same person (*ènìyàn*) to have more than one of these special abilities. Indeed, it is possible for the same person to have both the *àjẹ́* and the *àlùjànún*, as was indicated by quotation 22 above and by the following:

> (51) All of them [*àjẹ́*, *àlùjànún*, etc.] are *ènìyàn*, but they are different. There might be a person who was two [of the special types] simultaneously.

(52) There are some with two *èmí*. *Àjé* has two *èmí* . . . Those we regard as wise people have four *èmí*. The strongest *àlùjánún* has seven *èmí*, and every one [of the seven] has its own duty to perform. Someone with seven *èmí* will be more powerful than someone with [only] one. It's like someone who has many servants, because they can do much more work than someone with no servants.

This notion of multiple *èmí* presents a problem. For *if* it is the *èmí* that chooses a particular destiny (*orí*), is it then the case that a part of the *orí* of *àjé* is another *èmí*? It is one thing to say that the individual is presented with a number of different destinies from which he must make his choice, and quite another to say he is at the same time presented with a number of other vital spirits (*èmí*) from which he must also make his choice. The latter possibility introduces a latent inconsistency in that one is not clear how or why it is that certain *èmí* choose and certain *èmí* are chosen. Also one would wonder about the status or state of the consciousness of this second *èmí*, as it is referred to as in some sense external to the 'original' *èmí* of the person ('If I *have* the *àjé* . . .').

One possible solution to this apparent problem is to say that when the *onísègùn* speak of more than one *èmí*, it is not in the sense of literally adding a second, separate, conscious, spiritual unit to a first. Rather, in a somewhat metaphorical manner, what they are attempting to convey is that the choice of certain destinies will require that the *èmí* of a person develops additional *dimensions* (rather than *units* of 'spirituality'). As *àjé* a person's abilities and powers *are* greater than those of the ordinary person, and one way in which this is expressed in a somewhat figurative manner is by speaking of multiples of the original *èmí*.

(53) There is no person in the world with two *èmí*. We have only one. But these kinds of people [*àlùjànún, àjé*, etc.] have another special power (*àsè*) different from the ordinary power or ordinary person (*èniyàn*) which *Olórun* gives to everyone. The power of *àjé* is different; so also that of *emere*, from all other *èniyàn*. This special power is given by *Olórun*.

(54) All these types of people have only got one *èmí*. But they have another, special power (*àsè*). That is why we called them 'people with two bodies' (*abaraméjì*) in the olden days. Now we call them 'people who have got the power of darkness' (*agbára òkùnkùn*).

(55) If a person has these two powers (*àsè*) [i.e. *àjé* and *emèrè*], he can overcome any other person who is only one of them. Anyone who is both *àjé* and *emèrè* has three powers – the power of *àjé*, the power of *emèrè*, and the power of the ordinary *èniyàn*.

What this suggests is that the *onísègùn* conceive of the person initially as a basic, ordinary, spiritual component (*èmí/inú*) that, depending upon the destiny chosen, can expand into various dimensions of special abilities, talents, or powers. Different dimensions have different names because they involve different kinds of abilities or powers and even degrees of those powers. One basic, ordinary, spiritual component may develop into a number of extraordinary dimensions at the same time by taking on more than one of these abilities or powers in a single lifetime (*àlùjànún, àjé, emèrè*, etc.)

One task of a Yoruba philosophical psychology would therefore be to draw up a complete list of these various personality dimensions, of the powers associated with each, of the behaviour (if any) especially associated with each, and of the possible combinations. For it is possible that some cannot be combined in a single individual and it would be interesting to know why. It would also be interesting to know what percentage of people in Yoruba society actually do think of themselves as extraordinary, as enjoying one or more of these personality dimensions.

Is it, then, legitimate to treat *àjé*, etc., as Yoruba equivalents of personality-types? We would argue in favour of this, but only to a limited extent. The personality-types of professional psychology can be used to classify normal as well as abnormal behaviour or, in other words, can be applied in principle to every member of a society. These Yoruba types apply only to extraordinary persons, and therefore those who are capable of extraordinary actions. A second difference is that even if a person conceives of himself as *àjé*, it is not in the sense of it being the core of his self as is required by the definition of personality given on page 102 above. If the accounts of the *oníṣẹ̀gùn* are representative, the Yoruba person conceives of himself as a basic self (*ẹ̀mí*) that has endured and will endure through any number of lifetimes. He conceives of himself as a self that has certain special abilities or talents or attributes in this lifetime but that perhaps may not in the next. These abilities, then, even if his 'own' are somehow still external to the 'original' self that utilizes them. Therefore it seems more representative of Yoruba meaning to leave *àjé* as an *attribute* of the person rather than as a special *type* of person. Closer to the 'core' self than these abilities, or these extraordinary dimensions of the personality, is the *moral* self. For it is *ìwà* that is apparently the single most important factor influencing the choice of destiny and of the moral content of that destiny. And it is *ìwà* that apparently evolves and develops throughout the multiple lifetimes enjoyed by any person.

We have finally to deal with the 'problem' of secrecy. If the *àjé* can be a good person, a person who uses his extraordinary abilities for the benefit of mankind, why must he hide, why must he conceal them from the general public? One reason, of course, is the so-called popular stereotype of the *àjẹ́* as *ènìyàn burúkú*, as a bad person whose destiny is to cause harm and havoc to his or her fellow human beings. But, even if it is true that this is the attitude towards *àjẹ́* that is generated by this stereotype, one would be justified in asking why this stereotype has prevailed, why the good *àjẹ́* have not taken steps to draw attention to themselves.

At least one explanation of this is to appreciate the role of secrecy (*awo*) in such a situation. Extraordinary ability also demands extraordinary responsibility. The good *àjẹ́* recognizes that ordinary people cannot be expected to understand or to accomplish as much as he can. For this reason he cannot expect that, if he were to reveal his knowledge to them, they would use it responsibly and at the same time honour him as the intellectual and spiritual leader he would deserve to be. More likely, because the *basis* for his special abilities is something that *cannot* be shared or taught, ordinary people would come to fear him and take whatever steps they could to destroy him. So, even the good *àjẹ́* must conceal himself. He may still exercise his powers for the benefit of the community, but only in a deliberately indirect manner.

9. The Myth of Universal Theories

There is one final point about the activities of the *oníṣẹ̀gùn* with reference to the *àjẹ́* that should be made if our account is to be complete. This is that one of the professional activities of an *oníṣẹ̀gùn* who might have the *àjẹ́* is to identify, discipline, and sometimes destroy the power of other *àjẹ́* in the society. This need not be an anomaly if one keeps in mind the more basic distinction between *ènìyàn rere* (good persons) and *ènìyàn burúkú* (bad persons). For in general the *àjẹ́* for whom the *oníṣẹ̀gùn* is seeking (as *ènìyàn rere*) is *ènìyàn burúkú*, someone who has been identified as malevolent and a threat to the interests of the community.

The criticism could be made that in our presentation of the *àjẹ́* we give undue weight to the *àjẹ́* who are good persons and therefore misrepresent the numbers and influence of those who are bad. For, if the above phenomenon (the 'witch hunt') is a relatively common occurrence, then the Yoruba do indeed subscribe to the universal stereotype of the witch in a much more substantial manner than we have indicated.

Our reply would be to criticize the theories of African witchcraft we have considered for giving virtually *no* representation to the 'witch' who *is* a good person. And for this reason we conclude by asserting that 'witch' is not a representative translation of the meaning of '*àjẹ́*'. *Àjẹ́* are men. *Àjẹ́* is not quintessentially evil. *Àjẹ́* does make use of medicine. And, most importantly, *àjẹ́* may be a good person – intentionally benevolent, using their extraordinary talents for the welfare and benefit of mankind. Therefore, if scholars still wish to insist that witchcraft is some kind of conceptual and cultural universal, and that the Yoruba conform to it, we would suggest that they reflect upon the lessons to be learned from this chapter. For it may well be that many people who considered themselves to be witches *in the West* were also intentionally benevolent, exceptionally talented women *and* men who, because they constituted an implicit challenge to established ecclesiastical and judicial authorities, and to the established socio-economic order[32] (neither of which have been attributed by us to the *àjẹ́*), either successfully concealed themselves or were unfortunate enough to be reported, hunted down and exterminated. This would certainly help to explain why they were so scrupulous about leaving no written records or voluntary accounts of their activities.

What is responsible for the intellectual propensity to approach 'witchcraft' as a conceptual and cultural universal, if not what Quine earlier on termed the 'myth of universal propositions', here rephrased as the 'myth of universal theories'? The word in Yoruba may be *àjẹ́*, but the phenomenon to which it is used to refer is presumed to be the same.

No doubt scholars like Parrinder and Mair would disagree with any reference to their theories of a universal witchcraft as consequences of such a 'presumption'. They use methodologies derived from the social sciences, and they feel that the universality of their theories has been established on the basis of empirical research and evidence. But let us once again recall the manner in which these universal theories are generated.

Scholars of Western witchcraft complain that they are unable to provide a satisfactory analysis or explanation of it because of its historical remoteness and because of the bias and incompleteness of any evidential data that remains. Not being able to explain something would seem to imply that to a significant degree one also is not able to understand it. Such scholars therefore concentrate their interest upon Africa where, on the basis of careful fieldwork, African 'witchcraft' is proven to be a close replica of its Western counterpart and can therefore be used to provide the explanations of it that were hitherto lacking. But how can one conclude that two things are equivalent (Western witchcraft and African 'witchcraft') to the substantial degree required when one has first admitted that one does not really know or understand what one of them is?

If we follow Quine, one possible explanation for how this can happen is that such scholars *tend* to subscribe to (a myth of) universal theories (in this

---

[32]Summers repeatedly refers to them as heretics *and* anarchists (Summers 1973).

case, that witchcraft anywhere or in any historical period is essentially the same), and therefore do not give sufficient consideration to the possibility that something like *àjẹ́* may not fit the stereotype.

Quine's influence would lead us to suggest that one reason those characteristics shared in common by the Western stereotype of the witch and the Yoruba *àjẹ́* receive undue emphasis is because these are the characteristics of the witch that the Western scholar who undertakes fieldwork in Africa already has in mind. The process by which someone like Parrinder, for example, evolves his model is by borrowing from whatever culture whatever suits his purpose, which is to arrive at the universal model or theory. If Western witchcraft is not fully explicable, one can turn to its African 'equivalents'. But in doing so one carries along any number of the stereotypical characteristics of Western witchcraft and rediscovers them in Africa. One then returns to Western witchcraft with a full-blown, if culturally muddled, model which can now be used to illumine those hitherto murky and missing features of the phenomenon in the West that have eluded explanation or understanding. Everyone ends up sharing the same beliefs because from the beginning the (implicit) presumption was that everyone did share the same beliefs.

Parrinder adopts (on what *real* basis in the end, one wonders ?) Evans-Pritchard's model of Zande witchcraft as his most prominent theoretical universal and insists that it is representative of its Western counterpart(s). Consequently any Westerner who does not clearly make or observe a distinction between witchcraft and (magical) sorcery along the same lines is not just confused but mistaken. Similarly, African cultures (such as the Yoruba) and scholars of African 'witchcraft' who do not make the same distinction are also confused or mistaken about what they *really* mean. To be fair to Parrinder, he does assert that there are African societies that are exceptions to his universal model. *But the Yoruba are not supposed to be one.* Indeed, of all African peoples it is the Yoruba whom he has supposedly studied most carefully.

A final point for concern in a number of these analyses is the pejorative attitude adopted towards any culture that is thought to believe in what is said to be 'witchcraft'. The Western intellectual's attitude is more or less a 'Thank goodness we don't believe in *that* anymore', and that a society that does is primitive, sick and inhuman. But, as we have indicated, this pejorative attitude depends upon an incomplete, misleading, and therefore erroneous translation and definition of a term like the Yoruba *àjẹ́*.[33]

---

[33]For an interesting essay on the art of incomplete translations and definitions, of eliminating meanings that do not support the translator's purposes, see Gellner 1970.

Conclusion

At the very beginning we referred to the disrepute of African philosophy, and to the problematic relationship between it and what is commonly referred to as traditional African culture. Africans themselves are understandably wary of attempts to codify inherited thought systems into static cultural ideologies to which the name 'philosophy' is then appended. Attempts at 'analysing' African conceptual and belief systems, again in the name of philosophy, have produced speculative abortions that in the end so discredited the field that further attempts were discouraged. Consequently there are any number of examples of what African philosophy in relation to traditional thought should *not* be, and few of what it should be, at least in our opinion.

Is this a book on or of African philosophy? The question may seem redundant, but we think that it is not. In fact our answer to it must be carefully phrased: first, in terms of methodology and then of content. In the broadest sense the methodology we are applying is a variety of conceptual analysis, which is certainly an acceptable approach as far as contemporary academic philosophy is concerned. Where we run into a problem with some of our colleagues in African studies and in philosophy generally is over the issue of who is performing or is entitled to perform the analyses.

Philosophy has its own tradition of being a *second-order* discipline. This term too is given various definitions, but probably the most common is that the philosopher is a rather rare and also unique creature whose main task is to reflect upon ('analyse') and criticize things that most other people take for granted. A first-order discipline (let us take, for example, Christianity as represented by the Catholic Church) deals with ordinary mortals directly and gives them concrete advice on how to live their lives and solve their problems. A second-order (or philosophical) approach to Christianity or Catholicism would involve such topics as the kinds of reasons Christians give for something being true (let us take, for example, spiritual immortality) and a critique of them, both in terms of their logical consistency and empirical compatibility with other kinds of truths (scientific, for example). But the philosopher would not be expected, *qua* philosopher, to create a religion or to advise ordinary mortals on how to cope with their everyday problems.

The 'problem' referred to above, that has arisen from our work with the *oníṣẹ̀gùn* to date, arises from our supposed violation of this second-order convention in two respects. Firstly, in order to hold the discussions with them that we have had, we are doing fieldwork – going outside of academia and the university, into villages and people's homes, and in an embarrassingly empirical manner collecting information from them about what selected components of their conceptual system mean. This kind of first-order enterprise may be a task for the linguist or anthropologist, who are professionally trained for it. But it is not the sort of enterprise associated with philosophy or with the training one obtains from it as a discipline.

Secondly, our professional relationship with the *oníṣẹ̀gùn* is also subject to challenge. If we relate to them as colleagues (and they to us), as philosophers in their own right, can this be justified in view of the fact that they have undergone no professional training in philosophy? And, if this cannot be justified, then precisely what sort of relationship do we bear to them? If their role is reduced to that of informants, then once again we seem to have got ourselves involved in the kind of first-order enterprise the professional, academic philosopher should not undertake.

We argue that both of these objections arise from an insufficient appreciation of what it means to deal with an oral culture. Analytic philosophers who accept anthropologists' analyses of the professed knowledge of such cultures as 'traditional', as regarded and expressed in an uncritical and unreflective manner, tend to assign it insignificant philosophical status.

We maintain that the evidence and arguments of Chapter 2, in particular, challenge this. The Yoruba do not in general *regard* oral tradition as knowledge, as is evidenced by their classifying it as '*igbàgbọ́*' rather than as *imọ̀*'. The conditions or criteria they assign to it, and to second-hand information in general, indicate that it is regarded in a hypothetical and critical manner. Oral cultures, cultures that depend upon an oral *mode* for recording their beliefs, may express them in an apparently proverbial or unreasoned form due to considerations such as memorial economy. In other words, what an oral culture can afford to memorize may not be as much as what a literate one can afford to write down, and this may affect the manner in which information in the two cultures is recorded and expressed. But this need not imply that the intellectual attitudes maintained towards such information in the two sorts of cultures are also different.

If a culture maintains its abstract meanings and beliefs in an oral mode, and the academic philosopher decides to take an interest in them, there does not seem to be any other choice but for him to have face-to-face meetings with members of that culture. Exactly who would be the most appropriate members of that culture for him to meet is a question which we shall discuss later on. For the moment, surely this important if preliminary point may be acknowledged. Learning about oral cultures requires meeting with members of the cultures, for oral information comes out of mouths. Whether we went to meet the *oníṣègùn* in their homes, or whether they came to meet with us in the university (would this too have been 'fieldwork'?), was decided more out of considerations of diplomacy and mutual respect than of methodology (although meeting such people, relaxed and *in situ*, is somewhat easier).

We therefore argue that to refer to this kind of enterprise as 'fieldwork' is an unnecessary and misleading exaggeration. 'Fieldwork' is a technical term better reserved for anthropology, to accounts and analyses arising from the likes of participant observation, and so forth. We prefer the term 'collaborative analysis' to describe our own approach, but before we will be in a position to explain why, we must first take up the issue of who it is that is competent *to* analyse.

The stereotype of the uncritical, unreflective, 'closed' nature of African systems of thought has proved extraordinarily resilient and resistant to criticism. One obvious reason for this is that most of the evidence available supports it. To a limited extent we would agree. However, on the basis of the evidence we have collected, we are arguing that (at least) not all of Yoruba society fits the stereotype. And that we have 'discovered' this, leads us to suspect that our methodological approach differs in some important respects from those of other academic and professional disciplines that have a similar interest. We also believe that further applications of our methodological approach, by philosophers, may lead to other interesting discoveries, not only about the Yoruba thought system but about those of other African ethnic groups as well.

Some of our colleagues in philosophy in Africa have already arrived at an assessment of our approach (Oruka 1978; Bodunrin 1981) on the basis of previous methodological and research publications arising from this same research project. This assessment differs in several important respects from our own understanding of what we are doing.

In this assessment our approach has been awarded the rather unpalatable (euphoniously, at least) appellation of 'philosophical sagacity'. The most vigorous point of contention in the evaluation *of philosophical sagacity* stems from the following:

> It is one thing to show that there are men capable of philosophical dialogue in Africa and another to show that there are African philsophers in the sense of

those who have engaged in organized systematic reflections on the thoughts, beliefs and practices of their people.   (Bodunrin 1981: 170)

This distinction, between the sage who is able to make *some* contribution to philosophical discussion and the technical, analytic, academic philosopher coalesces with the following: 'the philosoper's approach to this study [African traditional culture and beliefs] must be one of criticism, by which one does not mean negative appraisal, but rational, impartial and articulate appraisal whether positive or negative.' (Bodunrin 1981: 173) And the ramification that: 'showing why a people hold a particular belief is not sufficient to show that the belief is rational.' (Bodunrin 1981: 175)

We said earlier on that the best way to answer the question about whether this is a book on African philosophy was to deal with it in terms of methodology and content. The above discussion, however incomplete, has concentrated upon methodology. We shall now make the transition to discussing the *content* of our work with the *onísègùn* because this is a better ground upon which to base a reply to this query about their philosophical capacities.

Let us first identify the level of analysis upon which we are working at present. Both Chapters 2 and 3 demonstrate that deeply rooted assumptions about the universality of meanings ('knowledge', 'belief', 'witch') and the correlative production of misrepresentative translations of Yoruba meanings said to refer to the 'same' things, have led to fundamentally false interpretations and analyses of Yoruba thought. In some cases these false interpretations have themselves been universalized and said to be representative of African thought in general.

African philosophy, insofar as it may come to deal with the analysis of African languages (or meanings) and evaluation of the beliefs of African cultures, will not even be in a position to begin until such things have been correctly understood and translated in a determinate manner. Part of the power of our exposition derives from the fact that it plays upon a dialectic between false and true meanings in translation; for example, the Yoruba being criticized for classifying certain kinds of information as knowledge when in fact they do not.

What we are doing with the *onísègùn*, therefore, is to begin the process of understanding Yoruba meanings anew. No important abstract meanings (we hope) are taken for granted because, as Quine has pointed out, this is often how misrepresentation arises. The detailed analyses of Yoruba meanings that constitute the heart of Chapters 2 and 3 were performed by the *onísègùn* as much or more than by us. We feel this is amply demonstrated by their statements. Discussions were 'led' in the sense that we usually would select the term we were interested in discussing and we would ask for clarifications of points that seemed obscure. But the *oníṣẹ̀gùn* with whom we are dealing do not take kindly to being asked leading questions. *They* are the authorities, and though they too respect us in our capacity as university lecturers, in the discussions our role is that of the intellectual gadfly who persists in raising questions that do not often arise in any society, and in reintroducing offshoots of them until our understanding and curiosity (as they see it) are satisfied.

We have never claimed that this role entitles them to be acclaimed philosophers, in the professional, academic sense. In these discussions we, as academic philosophers, also play a role, in that we usually choose the topic, introduce it, pursue it, write it up in systematic form, and compare it with purported counterparts in other conceptual systems. But none of this could take place without the *analytic* (as opposed to expository) contributions of the *oníṣẹ̀gùn*. The kinds of statements one finds in such numbered quotations as 20, 33, 38, 39, 40 and 46 in Chapter 2 go far beyond the domain of oral definition. They are clearly examples of an individual reflecting upon and analysing his own conceptual systen.

When it comes to the question of criticism in the sense of either the *oníṣẹ̀gùn* deliberately modifying or rejecting an element of the conceptual system because they find it inadequate, or deliberately creating and then comparing alternative concepts with a view to identifying the more satisfactory, there is only limited evidence of this kind of thinking in the material we have presented.

As far as the first alternative is concerned, evidence of this is found in those passages in which the *oníṣẹ̀gùn*, when explaining the criteria governing the application of a certain term, clearly appreciate the value of those criteria and the negative consequences of abandoning them (20, 33, 46 and 51). And they are not simply rationalizing. With reference to the second alternative this was, from the outset, a task we had assigned to ourselves. We hoped and have tried, once we had arrived at a reasonably deliberate understanding of a selection of abstract Yoruba meanings, to work out interesting comparisons with some of their English-language counterparts.

To return to 'philosophical sagacity'. The terms 'philosophy' and 'sage' are not, to our mind, compatible. The connotation of 'sage' is that of a wise man, but wise in the archaic ('traditional'?) sense of being knowledgeable about his people's beliefs, and not particularly or deliberately critical *of* them. If the philosopher's task is to analyse/criticize, there is then an element of inconsistency in conjoining the two.

To return to 'collaborative analysis'. By the word 'collaborative' we mean to emphasize the fact that the *oníṣẹ̀gùn*, explicitly, deliberately, and without being 'led', participate in the piecemeal analysis of their conceptual and thought system. In the literature generally classified under the heading 'African philosophy', one can go from the extreme of the 'sage' who undertakes the expression of an abstract system of thought *entirely* on his own to that of the alien observer who denies to an African people *any* significant powers of conceptual analysis and undertakes the process entirely on his own. Our own approach falls somewhere between the two. Both we and the *oníṣẹ̀gùn* participate in the process of analysis. They are men of keen intellect as well as of extraordinary practical skills. This is the basis upon which we work with them, and this is the sense in which we refer to them as our traditional colleagues.

We have still to come to terms with our original question about the relationship between this book and African philosophy. As the title indicates we regard the entire enterprise as an experiment, open to modification or revision in terms of both methodology and content. There is a certain deliberate irony in using Quine's indeterminacy thesis as a translation factor, as the intellectual device that eventually enables us to argue for genuine Yoruba conceptual alternatives. For it is with indeterminacy that he questions the feasibility of the entire translation exercise. Yet as we have said before, and as Quine himself admits, even if indeterminacy in translation on the abstract level may be contained, the profound sensitivity it generates to the possibility of alternative meanings is invaluable to the academic engaged in cross-cultural studies.

For something has happened. A category of information that was supposed to be 'knowledge' no longer is. People who were supposed to be 'witches' no longer are. From a cross-cultural point-of-view we therefore believe that this book introduces a new dimension into philosophy (not just into *African* philosophy) by demonstrating that the criteria governing the application of certain concepts in radically different language systems may be of genuine philosophical significance.[1] That propositional attitudes may be culturally relative is a fairly radical claim. But that is our claim, and we think that further *cross*-cultural conceptual comparisons will provide stronger evidence of the diversity, the relativity of meanings, than of that familiar godsend, propositional universality.

Two final suggestions. If the Yoruba have proven to be so conceptually

---

[1]"Irrespective of my thesis of indeterminacy of translation, your findings bring out interesting contrasts in the evidential connotations of these terms ['*mọ̀*' and '*gbàgbọ́*'].' (Quine, personal correspondence, 15 October, 1981)

distinctive, there is reason to suspect that other African conceptual systems maintain their own distinctive criteria as well. In which case it is time to dispense with the term 'African philosophy' when it is used to refer to some amorphous, pseudo-philosophical corpus of beliefs intellectually endemic to all African peoples. Secondly, we think it best to discontinue use of the word 'traditional' with reference to African systems of thought. Its use predisposes scholars to make certain assumptions that encourage mis-representations of African meanings and attitudes.

Enough said. This phase of the experiment is at an end. There is more work to be done.

Afterword: Indeterminacy, Ethnophilosophy, Linguistic Philosophy, African Philosophy

Barry Hallen

The discussion that follows concerns philosophical methodology or, better, methodologies. Most of the material that has been published to date under the rubric of African philosophy has been methodological in character. One reason for this is the conflicts that sometimes arise when philosophers in Africa attempt to reconcile their relationships with both academic philosophy and so-called African 'traditional' systems of thought. A further complication is that the studies of traditional African thought systems that become involved in these conflicts are themselves products of academia – of disciplinary methodologies.

Because of the emphasis placed upon these methodological ruminations, many of the methodological approaches to African philosophy that have been proposed have remained hypothetical or speculative – they have yet to be applied. One relevant difference about the methodology to be discussed below is that it has been 'tried and tested'. Whether it has also been proved 'true' is a subject still very much under discussion, and likely to remain so for some time.

1. Indeterminacy

The indeterminacy thesis was first proposed by W.V.O. Quine in 1960.[1] Over the years it has remained one of the more fiercely debated major-minor issues of contemporary philosophy. Its critics are numerous, and the critical interpretations and attempted refutations it has engendered compose a substantial body of literature.[2] Today its controversial status en-

Originally published in *Philosophy* 70 (1995): 377–393, and reprinted here by kind permission of the Royal Institute of Philosophy. The author is grateful to K. Anthony Appiah, Dorothy Emmet, Robin Horton, Valentin Mudimbe, W.V.O. Quine, and Olabiyi Yai for their comments on drafts of the original paper.

[1]In *Word and Object* (Quine 1960), Ch. 2 ('Translation and Meaning').

[2]A comprehensive bibliography of major interpretations, criticisms, elaborations, and defences of the indeterminacy thesis can be found in Kirk 1986: 259–265. For a much-quoted

dures, in no small part because of Quine's sustained efforts over the years to elaborate the thesis in a continuing dialogue with his critics.

Recasting the technical philosophical arguments of Quine's thesis into severely shortened, summary form can become a very masochistic undertaking. As the existing literature demonstrates, amply, this kind of strategy promotes caricature. The issues involved become more simplistic than is the case, and this tends to dramatize disproportionately some of the paradoxical, counterintuitive consequences of the thesis.[3]

I would prefer to concentrate here upon some of Quine's formative insights about the nature of language, the nature of meaning, and the relationships between languages that arise from the indeterminacy thesis. They too are controversial, and at best I hope to persuade you to 'try them on' as alternatives to our more conventional views of language and then to consider some of the interesting consequences that might follow for the translation of African 'beliefs' and abstract ideas.

1. Let us begin by regarding each natural language (English, Chinese, Yoruba, etc.) as a *unique* human creation that has its own intricate conceptual network(s) – ontological, epistemological, aesthetic, etc. – with distinctive semantic predispositions. Our immediate experience of the world is not self-explanatory or neatly categorized. It is humankind, by means of its creative genius, that invents languages and imposes empirical and theoretical order on that experience.

2. Let us also suspend our tendency to assume that in their heart of hearts all of our languages share a common group of *universal meanings*

'informal' discussion of Quine's thesis by many of the principals involved (including Quine), remarkable for its plain talk about complex philosophical issues, see Davidson et al., 1974.

[3]In the literature on African philosophy, the earliest reference to the indeterminacy thesis that I have been able to identify occurs in a footnote to Henri Maurier, 'Do We Have an African Philosophy?' in the 2nd edition, published in 1979, of *African Philosophy: An Introduction*; see Wright (ed.) 1984. Interestingly, the footnote is editorial—i.e., it was added by Wright—and contains an explicit recommendation that the issues raised by Quine's thesis should warrant the special interest of African philosophers. More generally, one of the earliest analytic philosophers to recognise and enunciate clearly the theoretical potential of African languages for African philosophy, a position he has continued to refine up to the present day, is Kwasi Wiredu. See Wiredu 1972: 11.

I am indebted to Robin Horton for first drawing my attention to Quine's indeterminacy thesis and for many valuable conversations about translation. For his collected thoughts on the subject, which should by no means be treated as his final word, see Horton 1993.

There was substantial discussion of the indeterminacy thesis in the philosophy of the social sciences and in anthropology before it became an issue for African philosophy. A particularly informative interdisciplinary collection can be found in Hollis and Lukes (eds.) 1982.

or *propositions*. By 'universal propositions' Quine refers to the belief that while the word for 'destiny' may be different in Yoruba from what it is in English, the underlying meaning is the same. Quine's view is not, specifically, a defense of relativism. It is a critique of the idea that we have any direct 'experience' of universal meanings.[4]

3. A belief in the universality of meanings may be of empathic value to someone who is a stranger to another language-culture, or of heuristic value to the lexicographer devising a bilingual dictionary, but it tends to negate the possibility of uniqueness that we began with. It can also be said to promote a form of *ethnocentrism*, in that translators who believe in universal propositions, or do translation between two languages as if there were universal propositions, will likely favour the meanings of their own natural language (English, for example), effectively universalizing them into propositions, and then proceed to impose English meanings upon other languages via the process of translation.

4. Let us also suspend our conventional notion of '*meaning*'. When an English-language translator sets out to communicate with an alien, the psychological predispositions of her own language may subliminally persuade her to conceive of the 'inner' alien person as a mind, as a consciousness inhabiting a body. They may also persuade her to presume that consciousness contains the meanings she needs to 'reach' and to 'study' in order to formulate accurate translations of the alien language. Worse still, she may be deceived into thinking that the translations of alien meanings that she eventually does propose derive their accuracy from the fact that they really do *correspond* to 'meanings' in the alien mind.

In fact, we never have direct access to another consciousness. What we do have direct access to are alien words coming out of alien mouths. Strictly from a *methodological* point of view, therefore, it is deceptive for the translator to operate in anything other than a *behaviouristic* universe.[5]

5. Familiarity with an alien language on the relatively empirical level is not sufficient to enable us to predict the nature of *alien theoretical or abstract beliefs*. The gap between the accidental spilling of salt and the beliefs that interpret it as bad luck is vast.

6. The hopes for objectivity, for proof of *accuracy in translation*, dif-

---

[4]J.J. Katz compares the effects of Quine's critique of meaning to those of Hume's sceptical analysis of causality in 'The Refutation of Indeterminacy' (Katz 1988).

[5]For the purpose of this discussion it is enough to say that the form of behaviourism being introduced is *methodological*, as opposed to the reductive psychological species enunciated by Skinner and Co. Quine is not denying the existence of the conscious 'mental' self, of personal feelings, or of introspection. But these experiences are private to each individual rather than public.

fer substantially between the relatively empirical ('It is raining') and the abstract ('Truth is beauty'). Translations of empirical statements are susceptible to a degree of public, verifiable testing of meaning. Theoretical abstractions are relatively *im*material in character. Translation on the abstract level is accordingly much more difficult to control or to verify.

7. The translator who is *bilingual* is not excepted from these problems. She may be perfectly fluent in each of the languages that are targeted by a particular bilingual translation. But when she begins to affirm that a certain term 'extracted' from one of the languages means precisely the same as a certain term in the other language, she is still imposing the meanings of the one language's conceptual network upon the other in hypothetical fashion.

8. Any extended translation process between two languages – as found, for example, in a work of cultural anthropology or a bilingual dictionary – is an elaborate, interrelated network constructed of innumerable hypotheses that stipulate the meanings of English-language words as equivalent to alien-language words. Each definition of an alien word becomes, in effect, an *interpretation* rather than a translation, a working hypothesis, a rendering based upon a network of other translated renderings. Looking at things from this perspective makes manifest the approximate nature of the entire process. It also raises the possibility that another translator could come along who would disagree with the schema worked out by her predecessor and introduce an alternative schema, an alternative interpretation, that differed in important respects, and therefore would produce a different version of the 'African beliefs' in *translation*.

9. What *objective criteria* can one appeal to in order to determine which alternative translation is determinate – is closest to the 'true' (alien) meanings? There are none that would be sufficient. This, admittedly in castrated form, is the point of the indeterminacy thesis.

Quine *is not* advocating a ban on translation, nor is he implying that published studies of African abstract beliefs that are based upon translations of African languages are false. Quine *is* advocating a degree of *scepticism* about *purportedly* rigorous, objective, detailed analyses of alien abstract ideas *in translation*. Once one recognizes the weakness of the empirical constraints placed upon the communication of meanings between two languages that may historically have no cause to share a single common cognate, what exactly is the *objective* basis upon which we assign virtually literal accuracy to theoretical translations?

From the standpoint of indeterminacy, studies of African abstract meanings in translation are built upon a more fragile basis of interpretation than their rhetoric implies. This needs to be recognized more widely than it is

– especially when such studies serve as an empirical basis for attributing oddities in reasoning and/or theoretical understanding to an African conceptual system. A prelogical mentality *could be* the creation of a prelogical translation. One who is persuaded by the possibility of indeterminacy would prefer that we be more flexible, more open to the possibilities of misrepresentation, of approximation by translation, especially on the level of abstract thought. On this level there may be no such thing as literal translation. Everything becomes free translation, interpretation.

In the *absence* of secure objective criteria for determining which translation schema is more accurate, Quine proposes several translation guidelines that he thinks may at least reduce the risks of producing translations of African meanings that are offensive as well as indeterminate.[6]

Some consequences of these alternative criteria would be as follows. One would become suspicious of translations of African meanings that propose to assign a *plurality of meanings* to the same term in an African conceptual system. A translator might justify such a practice by saying that these are dependent upon the circumstances or the context in which the term is used. Given indeterminacy, an alternative reason *could* be that translators have tactical recourse to context-dependent meanings because they – perhaps unwittingly/unknowingly – have been *unsuccessful* in coming up with a *determinate* meaning. In effect, then, the translator attributes her own confusion to the alien conceptual system. This makes the aliens appear somehow exotic or bizarre when in fact the real culprit is the translation.

Suspicion should also be focused upon cases in which the African is made to mean something empirically bizarre and inappropriate to a situation's common-sense circumstances. This may indicate a situation in which inadequate translation results in Africans apparently affirming transparently false statements and therefore becoming less than rational. Given indeterminacy, an alternative explanation could be that there are problems in the conceptual translation network that cause African meanings to take on apparent absurdity in the language of translation.

To conclude: Quine is not saying that people are always rational. His *scepticism* about the entire process of translating the meanings from one language into another moves him to caution us that we have *as good reason* to suspect our systems of translation as we do to suspect the African of being responsible for apparently exotic, bizarre, or irrational statements in any given context.

Quine 1960: 73–79; see also pp. 30–34, above.

2. Ethnophilosophy

'Ethnophilosophy' is a four-letter word, an intellectual's invective. I don't know of anyone in African philosophy today who voluntarily identifies themselves as an 'ethnophilosopher'. It is a category invoked by a critic when he wants to express disapproval of the work of someone in African philosophy.

The term was originally coined in 1970 by Paulin Hountondji, a philosopher from the Republic of Bénin.[7] He uses it to characterize the work of people like Placide Tempels (1959), Alexis Kagamé (1956), Léopold Sédar Senghor (1964), Marcel Griaule (1965), and Germain Dieterlen (1951). His intention is to condemn the intellectual injustice that he believes to be enshrined in publications purporting to be African *philosophy* when they display the following characteristics:

(1) Ethnophilosophy presents itself as a philosophy of *peoples* rather than of *individuals*. In Africa one is therefore given the impression that there can be no equivalents to Socratic philosophy or Kantian philosophy. Ethnophilosophy speaks only of Bantu philosophy, Dogon philosophy, Yoruba philosophy; as such its scope is collective, of the world-view variety.

(2) Ethnophilosophy's *sources* are in the past, in what is described as authentic, *traditional* African culture of the *pre*-colonial variety, of the Africa prior to 'modernity'. These can be found primarily in products of *language*: parables, proverbs, poetry, songs, myths – oral literature generally.

(3) From a *methodological* point of view ethnophilosophy therefore tends to present African beliefs as things that do not change, that are somehow timeless. Disputes between ethnophilosophers arise primarily over how to arrive at a correct *interpretation* of historical traditions.[8] African systems of thought are portrayed as placing minimal emphasis upon rigorous argumentation and criticism in a search for truth that provides for

---

[7]'Remarques sur la philosophie africaine contemporaine', *Diogenes* 71 (1970); revised and translated in Hountondji 1983, Ch. 1 ('An Alienated Literature').

[8]There is anticipation of *indeterminacy* in the following remarks from Hountondji, in which he derides the usually unspecified methods used by these ethnophilosophers to educe African philosophy from oral literature: 'The discourse of ethnophilosophers, be they European or African, offers us the baffling spectacle of an imaginary interpretation with no textual support, of a genuinely "free" interpretation, inebriated and entirely at the mercy of the interpreter, a dizzy and unconscious freedom which takes itself to be *translating* a text which does not actually exist and which is therefore unaware of its own *creativity*. By this action the interpreter disqualifies himself from reaching any *truth* whatsoever, since truth requires that freedom be limited, that it bow to an order that is not purely imaginary and that it be aware both of this order *and* of its own margin of creativity' (1983: 189, in note 16).

discarding the old and creating the new. Tradition somehow becomes anti-thetical to innovation.

If this material had been presented as cultural anthropology or as ethnology Hountondji would have no objection to it. But when it is introduced as philosophy, as *African* philosophy, a demeaning and subversive double standard is introduced that excuses African philosophy from having critical, reflective (it becomes, in effect, *prereflective*), rational, scientific, and progressive content in any significantly cross-culturally comparative sense.

Hountondji does not hold these perpetrators of an unauthentic African philosophy *personally* responsible for their crimes. In their day in their own intellectual circles they believed they were doing something revolutionary, something genuinely radical and progressive, by daring to link the word 'philosophy' directly to African systems of thought.

Also, Hountondji appreciates the difficult circumstances of Africa's intellectual history during the colonial period. Academic philosophers – African or expatriate – were a rare species. The principal initiatives for serious scholarly studies of African cultures came from ethnography and anthropology. Given the holistic parameters of the social sciences, it is understandable – if still not ideologically acceptable – that these early ethnophilosophers began to approach the subject of African philosophy on such a collectivized, tribalized scale.[9]

3. Linguistic Philosophy

As an academic philosopher who had become interested in the translation of abstract African meanings, I was naturally drawn to some of the promising work that has been done this century in the *philosophy of language*. Since a good deal of philosophy is devoted to the study of problems for which no standardized solution has been found, the philosophical perspectives on problems of translation are diverse. Quine's indeterminacy thesis is only one example of this diversity.

There is a cluster of philosophers and of philosophical 'movements' in twentieth-century academic philosophy that, by prescription or example, place a premium on *description*.[10] Although many of these philosophers

---

[9]For a postmodern defense of ethnophilosophy, see Salemohamed 1983. For a more recent, comparatively strident condemnation of virtually the whole of 'African philosophy' as *non*-philosophy, as too culturally specific and descriptive (in other words, as ethnophilosophy yet again), see Pearce 1992.

[10]Most prominently the phenomenological movement. For a discussion of phenomenological description and African philosophy, see Hallen 1976.

preferred the terms '*analysis*' or '*analytic philosophy*' for describing their efforts, in effect that meant a form of minute, painstaking description. For some it was the description of language *usage* (as in the cases of the later Wittgenstein and J.L. Austin). For others it was the beliefs and the conceptual contents of common sense (Gilbert Ryle). These efforts were approaching a kind of intellectual crescendo in 1959 with the publication of Sir Peter Strawson's book, *Individuals* (1959). This was said to be an exercise in 'descriptive metaphysics', which meant something like detailed analyses of the meanings of primordial concepts in the English language, such as 'bodies' and 'persons'.

It is possibly unfair to characterize these traditions in contemporary philosophy as a Western species of *ethnophilosophy* – if for nothing else because of the very specific terms of reference Hountondji has in mind for his criticisms. But the emphasis placed upon '*mere description*' as an alternative to critical argumentation, and the concentration upon *language* (as assimilated by written rather than oral cultures) *as used* and *everyday meanings* and *beliefs* indicate that certain essential attributes are held in common.

* * *

My own primary concerns were *methodological*, instrumental. I was in need of practical techniques for the study of concepts or abstract meanings. The most important criterion for adoption was that they might be useful in the African context.

I was not concerned – at this initial stage – to become involved in the more profound disputes over the nature of language, of meaning, of reference, or of language's role in the posing of philosophical problems. Given the disrepute of ethnophilosophy and the general lack of technical philosophical content in anthropological literature,[11] there was an obvious need for some *first-order* work – collection, analysis, and systematization of African conceptual meanings – by scholars with philosophical sensitivities.

In the course of my methodological borrowings, in a thoroughly eclectic manner, I intermixed insights and techniques from different 'schools' of thought that are normally not regarded as compatible – from positivism (Quine) and from ordinary-language philosophy (J.L. Austin) for example. I found some of Austin's procedures for the collection and analysis of meanings[12] plausibly practical for the African context. Deliberately adapted rather than merely adopted, and as amended, they may be summarized as follows:

---

[11] Anthony Appiah makes a similar observation about anthropology in *In My Father's House* (1992: 94). Robin Horton is, of course, one distinguished exception.

[12] As reconstructed with greater technical precision by J.O. Urmson (1969).

(1) Select a *field of discourse* in an African language to concentrate analysis upon, preferably one that is related to the concerns of academic philosophy.

(2) Collect all *vocabulary* that may be relevant to this subject-area.

(3) For collecting such information it is better to work with a *group* of indigenes, more or less as colleagues, rather than as an independent researcher:
– this is particularly helpful when dealing with a culture that is significantly oral;
– it is also helpful to any principal researcher who is targeting a language that is not their own first language.

(4) The different members of the group must somehow all agree to accept the *same general methodological approach* to the research.

(5) Collect and/or construct *'paradigm cases'* or examples of situations where this vocabulary is used in the correct way.

(6) Also pay attention to examples of *wrong usage* – where the terms should not apply.

(7) Again with reference to the examples of usage, amplify the *meanings* of key terms on the basis of *extensive discussions* with one's indigenous colleagues (this point might pain Austin).

(8) As much as possible, pay special attention to the empirical conditions, criteria, and content of each term. In some cases these may be sufficient to make one alternative translation of a theoretical term preferable to another (even if, according to Quine, this 'preferable' translation ultimately also remains indeterminate).

(9) Do *library research* on what other scholars (philosophers, anthropologists, linguists, ethnologists) may have had to say about this specific field of discourse in whatever African language you have chosen. Also enquire about directly comparable studies in the same or some other natural language.

(10) Resist *wholesale importation* of academic philosophical theories as vehicles for the explication of African meanings. Careless application of a technical vocabulary can skew sensibilities and create confusion.[13]

I suppose a good deal of this might seem carelessly informal to the trained professional linguist. The most I can say to justify this approach is that it seems to have produced some interesting results. For example, in connection with Yoruba-language translations, one area of discourse that proved of interest was what in academic philosophy corresponds to epistemology, or the theory of knowledge.[14] In plain talk this would encompass the vocabulary and the criteria used by the Yoruba to evaluate and to grade any type of information – as from less to more credible.

---

[13]Appiah gives an example of this with reference to Cartesian dualism (1992: 100), a theoretical parallel frequently drawn in contemporary African philosophy.
[14]See Ch. 2, above.

4. African Philosophy

In 1975 no philosophy department syllabus in Nigeria listed a course in African philosophy. At the University of Ife the department did, however, offer a course in African Traditional Thought. This nomenclature – 'traditional thought' rather than 'philosophy' – reflects the indirect but fundamental influence that anthropology for long exerted upon the relationship between academic philosophy and Africa.

My aim is neither to criticise nor to censure my ethnographic colleagues. It was never a part of anthropology's brief to suppress African philosophy. Nevertheless, the assessments made of African 'modes of thought' in anthropological studies did not encourage the interest of academic philosophers in their theoretical intellectual potential. Characteristics such as non-critical, prereflective (associated with being 'traditional'), non-reasoned (associated with being 'emotive', 'symbolic'), non-individualized (associated with being 'tribal') are symptomatic. This assessment was a further formative influence upon *ethnophilosophy*. The reported relative absence of an articulate and analytically reflective intellectual tradition in African systems of thought inclined those in search of African philosophy to seek it in alternative sources, such as myths and proverbs.

The stereotype of the African intellect that arose from these anthropological studies created serious problems for linking a philosophy syllabus to Africa's indigenous cultural base. For Africa was not introduced to academic philosophy as an unknown: the problem was not simply a lack of information about African traditional modes of thought. The problem was that the subcontinent's indigenous intellectual attributes appeared to be virtually diametrically opposed to critical thought as defined by academic philosophical tradition.[15]

Some African philosophers have responded to this apparent dilemma by arguing, astutely, that it was based upon an *unfair comparison* between widespread popular beliefs (so-called 'folk philosophy') in Africa and theories that were the product of deliberately intense and highly sophisticated research (science, philosophy) in the West. Western cultures were gradually coming to terms with negative elements of their own folk philosophies (superstitions, etc.) on the basis of reasoned assessments and consensus. The more practical course for Africa would be for her peoples to deal with their popular beliefs in an analogous fashion.[16] The problem

---

[15]An opinion that unfortunately is still all too common. This same sentiment is echoed by Appiah: 'That African philosophy just is ethnophilosophy has been largely assumed by those who have thought about what African philosophers should study' (1992: 94).

[16]The original debate about this issue may be found in Horton 1967 (reprinted in Horton

with this response is that it does not effectively counter the claim,[17] supposedly itself scientific, that on a more primordial level than popular beliefs Africa's intellectual predispositions – including those underlying the conceptual networks used to articulate African abstract or theoretical ideas – are quintessentially symbolic, emotive, and prereflective in nature.

When my colleague Olubi Sodipo and I agreed to join forces for a philosophical investigation of Yoruba epistemological discourse, using the indeterminacy thesis as a foil, we anticipated complaints from our colleagues in both anthropology and philosophy. We expected them to accuse us of behaving too much like anthropologists – doing something very like fieldwork – when professionally we were qualified only as academic philosophers.

What we did not anticipate was that, because of our extensive efforts to re-present Yoruba meanings in analytic, systematic, and somewhat determinate form, they would be characterized by several critics as 'mere description' or 'merely descriptive' and thus branded a further example of *ethnophilosophy*.[18]

Such labelling is misguided, and is only made possible by yanking the Yoruba material out of its wider context and treating it in isolation from the discussion about meaning and problems of translation. For the point of the entire Hallen-Sodipo translation exercise is to test Quine's thesis by *exploring the limits of determinate translation* (into English) with reference to a cluster of reasonably abstract concepts (from Yoruba) that are relevant to the theory of knowledge.

1993); and Wiredu, 'How Not to Compare African Traditional Thought with Western Thought', in Wiredu 1980. See also Hallen 1977; Appiah 1992, Ch. 6 ('Old Gods, New Worlds').

[17]'The real difficulty encountered in the understanding of primitive thought is not', as some philosophers suppose, that its 'supernatural' beliefs are refractory to rational understanding, but that symbolism is linguistically untranslatable and its ideas encapsulated in action, ritual, and social institutions; that is, they exist at a sub-verbal level' (Hallpike 1979: 485). See also McClean 1994.

[18]Peter Bodunrin, in an article that remains controversial among both friends and foes of African philosophy, was the first to criticise my work for its ethnophilosophical tendencies. But as this early criticism was made of a paper entitled, with deliberate precaution, 'A Philosopher's Approach to Traditional Culture' – rather than 'Traditional Philosophy' – I think it was premature (although valuable nonetheless). See Hallen 1975; Bodunrin 1981.

Hallen and Sodipo, individually and collectively, are explicitly associated with ethnophilosophy in Bello 1988; Oruka, 'Philosophic Sagacity in African Philosophy', in Oruka (ed.) 1990; and Oseghare 1992. Four reviews of the original edition of *Knowledge, Belief, and Witchcraft* that discuss its wider philosophical horizons (Quine, indeterminacy, translation, etc.) in a comprehensive manner are Byrne 1987; Cordwell 1987; Jorion 1987; and Mudimbe 1987.

When viewed from such a perspective, the exercise is certainly of philosophical substance. It is also crucial to the entire enterprise of African philosophy. For African philosophy, insofar as it may deal with the *analysis* of African languages (or meanings) and the *evaluation* of African beliefs expressed in these languages, will not even be in a position to *begin* until we are assured that such meanings can be correctly understood and translated in a reasonably determinate manner.

A second argued consequence of this translation enterprise concerns the *challenge posed to the evidential status* of that troublesome stereotype of traditional African systems of thought that has been inherited via ethnography, and that has for long obstructed the academic philosopher's dialogue with African cognitive systems. I can only summarize here in a most unsatisfactory manner, but the first results of the Hallen-Sodipo approach[19] began from the knowledge-belief distinction as portrayed in English-language philosophical analysis and explicitly set out to investigate whether there was anything comparable to it in Yoruba discourse. Initiating our topical study of Yoruba discourse from this special interest of Western epistemology was deliberate. The characterisation of traditional discourse, as defined by the West, effectively portrays it as lacking critical epistemological content. Yet the conceptual network that emerges from our analyses of Yoruba meanings is by comparison markedly critical, sceptical, and empirical in character. In fact, it proved so out of line with what one was led to expect by the stereotype of 'traditional thought' that initially we queried our own conclusions and searched anew for possible underlying *mis*-translations, *mis*-representations. That there do indeed prove to be a selection of subtle, different, yet interestingly comparable Yoruba epistemic criteria introduces a viable way of doing analytic philosophy into Africa.

Quine's remonstrances about re-fashioning alien thought systems according to one's own cultural 'images' was one source of caution here. The Western academic philosopher has been schooled in very specific traditions of 'rationalism' and, at the same time, conditioned to place a high value upon aspects of empirical testing and verification. The two combined could influence him to inflate approximate references in Yoruba discourse to anything resembling either far beyond their true significance.

Indeed, it was a continuing awareness of the pitfalls of indeterminacy and possible *mis*-interpretations that persuaded us not to treat our English-language translations of Yoruba meanings *immediately* as reliably repre-

---

[19]As published in the original edition of the present work; see Ch. 2, above.

sentative. In the original edition of *Knowledge, Belief, and Witchcraft*, we made an appeal for corrective criticisms from other Yoruba scholars.[20] It seemed advisable to do this lest these meanings be consolidated into a further false orthodoxy that would further mislead people about the nature of African 'thought'.

I now think sufficient time has passed that we can be assured of a reasonable consensus. Our model of the conceptual network has passed some kind of test. The general structure remains intact.[21] It is time to move on.

To what, one may ask? The task embraced by academic philosophy is two-fold: to *understand* (let it serve here as another expression for 'to describe') and to assess. Philosophy is not a science, and the solutions it offers may not be so convincing that a targeted problem is finally resolved. But that does not absolve the academic philosopher from a responsibility to consider the *evidence* and *argumentation* in favour of each of the various alternative systems of understanding – for example, of each of the conceptual networks constitutive of the various natural languages in our world – and then try to determine which among them are the better instruments for understanding, the more empirically convincing or (to put it most imposingly) true.

Another alternative would be to opt for relativism – the relativity of truth – and argue that because what the Yoruba find true may not be what the English find true, there are many truths and there the matter rests. Accurate *descriptions* or the cataloguing of the various systems of conceptual understanding in the world would then become all that is required. This might also seem to be a consequence of indeterminacy, but, as the thesis is presented here, it does not follow. The problems in capturing the meanings of one conceptual system with the meanings of another need not imply that both may be true.

Judging the truth of the conceptual systems of the world's various *natural* languages in terms of any absolute criterion (which itself would have to be expressed in language) might seem a preposterous enterprise.[22] But if reduced to more manageable proportions – such as, for example, the relative merits and demerits of different systems of epistemological concepts

---

[20]See p. 83, above: 'We would be pleased if the response to this chapter generates information about additional empirical content that may lead to even more determinate translations'.
[21]Reviewing the earlier edition of the present work, A.G.A. Bello (1988) made a number of suggestions for revisions of our Yoruba translations, which we have taken note of.
[22]A great deal has been done in this regard with artificial languages, but the connection between artificial and natural languages remains a subject of dispute. For an early but still seminal analysis of this debate, see Katz and Fodor 1962.

and criteria when judged as instrumental tools – it does not seem so impossible.[23]

At this point I would opt for, as a further step towards responsible cross-cultural comparative research in African philosophy, aiming at a better understanding of *why* a specific conceptual network with its peculiar (possibly unique) conceptual components may be suited to a particular African cultural context. The conceptual network of any natural language does not explain or justify itself in the didactic argumentative manner that has become conventional to academic philosophy. Such reasons must be educed from a language by siting it[24] in its wider cultural and social contexts. Some may object that this sounds more like the sociology of language than philosophy, but it is another facet of that comprehensive understanding academic philosophers are obliged to attempt before they pass comparative judgements.[25]

5. Conclusion

I appreciate that many of the suggestions and admonitions I have expressed may already be incorporated into the methodologies and research activities of other disciplines involved with African studies. Nevertheless, one role of the indeterminacy thesis in African *philosophy* can be to sensitize those committed to dealing with the translation and assessment of abstract ideas on the basis of cross-cultural comparisons to the limitations of conceptual networks generally for the representation and analysis of alien meanings. And this caution should extend as much to African interpretations of Western meanings as to Western interpretations of African meanings.

One of Hountondji's complaints about ethnophilosophy is that its focus is collective, tribalized rather than defined in terms of the views of individual African thinkers. Adapting linguistic philosophy as a methodological basis for African philosophy should qualify it as an exception to this criticism. Linguistic philosophy is concerned with the study of languages,

---

[23]In *Belief, Language, and Experience*, Rodney Needham discusses the limitations of the English-language concept 'belief' as a vehicle for cross-cultural translations. See Needham 1972.

[24]Possibly imaginatively, as Quine does in the radical translation experiment he uses to introduce the indeterminacy thesis.

[25]J.T. Bedu-Addo makes a perceptive cross-cultural comparison of the significance of knowledge via direct experience (what has become known as 'knowledge by acquaintance' in academic philosophy) and its roots in orality in the Greek, Akan, Yoruba, and Latin languages. See Bedu-Addo 1983: 232–233, especially note 13. See also Appiah 1992: 98.

and languages function as means of communication on the basis of shared meanings.

The technical, philosophical analysis of African conceptual networks can hopefully be of a more rigorous methodological order than the classic studies that somehow 'extract' a so-called traditional system of thought from the oral literature of an African culture. Whether, interior to an African language, there is a special vocabulary, a unique form of conceptual network, or a particular form of discourse that is somehow peculiar to whatever is defined as the 'traditional' is a possibility that invites further – what else? – philosophical analysis.

Appendix: Yoruba Quotations for Chapter Two

This is a book that has some things to say about translation, and the various problems that may be involved in finding meaning equivalents or alternatives in one language for those of another. We have therefore decided to include the original statements made to us by the *oníṣègùn*, in Yoruba, as additional evidence for those with sufficient knowledge of the two languages to judge the adequacy (in terms of *meanings*) of our translations.

The numbers of the statements in Yoruba correspond to the numbers of the statements (in English) in the text of Chapter Two. We would have liked to include the same series of quotations, in Yoruba, for Chapter Three, but for reasons of space this has not proved possible.

(1) Èyí tí o fi ojú ara rẹ̀ rí tì ọkọ̀n rẹ jẹ́ ọ lẹ́ri pé o ṣe òótọ́ yẹn ni ó dára jù.

(2) Ó dá mi lójú. Èyí ni pé mo rí ẹrí òótọ́ ní ó ṣe kin ní yì . . . Ó ti dá ẹ lójú.

(3) Èyí tí o rí yẹni ni ó dára jù.

(4) Tí o bá rí kin ni kan, tí o bá rùn ní igbà kin ni ati igbà kéjì tí o bá ti mọ̀ pé òun ni tí o ba dẹ̀ ti gbòòrùn rẹ nigbà míràn wà a mo nkan náà, nítorí o ti mọ o tẹ́lẹ̀ tí o bá jẹ́ wípé igbà kan ni o gbọ kòile ye, á sáà mọ̀ pé nkankan nrun.

(5) Bí o bá mọ́ọ̀, o ti mọ nkan tí òun fi síbẹ̀ ni. Tí mo dijú tí mo sì fi ọwọ́ kan àrọ yì, mo ti mọ̀ pe àrọ ni. Nítorípé mo ti mọ̀ tẹ́lẹ̀.

(6) Tí o kò ba ri, o fi ọwọ́ kan lásán. Nítorípé ènìyàn ti a ò mọ̀ tẹ́lẹ̀ bí a fi ọwọ́ kan a kò lè mọ̀ ọ́.

(7) O ti mọ̀ pé 'cupboard' ni eléyì, bí ènìyàn nsọ pé kò kì nṣe 'cupboard', èmi yí o tẹnu mọ̀ pé 'cupboard' ni nkan tí mo mọ̀ daadaa, ẹrí ọkọ̀n ti jẹ́ ọ pé òun ni; igò funfun yì, bi wọn sọ pe dúdú ni, o ti mọ dáadáa pé funfun ni. Ìwọ yi o so wípé funfun ni, ó ti dámilójú pé funfun ni, mo mọ̀, mo mọ̀ pé funfun ni.

(8) Èyí ni pé kò jẹ́ o ní ẹrí ọkọ̀n pé òun ni, ẹrí ọkọ̀n kò jẹ́ ọ. Ìgbàtí o bá rí ohun tí ọkọ̀n rẹ sọ. Ti o kò ṣe iyè méji.

(9) Nwọn lè ní kí o kálọ kí ẹnìkan. Ìwọ lè sọ wípé bí ó bá jẹ wípé ilé lágbájá ni ẹ nlọ iwọ kò lọ. Ẹ̀rí ọkọ̀n rẹ ni ó sọ fún ọ kí o má ṣe lọ. Tí wọn bá fà ẹ́ kí ẹ dé'bẹ̀ kí ìjà ṣẹlẹ̀, wà a sọ pé njẹ́ o ò ti sọ pé o kò lọ? Pé ẹ̀rí ọkọ̀n rẹ ti sọ fún ẹ pé kò yẹ kí o lọ. Ẹ̀rí ọkọ̀n ẹni ni ó ma nsọ pé bóyá nkan dára tàbí kò dára, èyí sì ṣe pàtàki ju àmọ̀ràn ẹnikẹ́ni. Bí ẹ̀rí ọkọ̀n rẹ bá bá ẹ sọ̀rọ̀ eni tí ó wá yío lórí padà yẹn kí ó tó yíẹ yio pẹ́.

(10) Tí mo bá fẹ́ràn rẹ ẹ̀rí ọkọ̀n mi yío má sọ fún mi bí o kò ti lẹ̀ sí níbẹ̀, bí mo bá sẹẹ́ ní ikà, tí mo sì ri ẹ tí nkò kí ẹ ṣùgbọ́n ẹ̀rí ọkọ̀n mi sọ fún mi pé èmi kò fẹ́ràn rẹ.

(11) Òótọ́ ni ọkọ̀ yì dúró sí ibí yí bi o sọ pé kò dúró, wàá sọ pe ẹ fi ojú ara rẹ ri pé òótọ́ lo dúró kò yẹ ki o ṣe iyè méjì.

(12) Tí a bá nṣe nkan nísìyí, òmìràn lè já sí òfo, òmìrán lè já sí òótọ́ ni ọ̀rọ̀ tí a nṣo yi, olúkúlùkù ni o ni ẹ̀bùn ọ̀rọ̀ sísọ, ẹlòmíràn irọ́ pípá elòmíràn òtitọ̀ ṣíṣẹ. Nígbàti ó ba ti nṣe, óṣeéṣe kó jẹ́ pé ó purọ́, ó ṣeéṣe ki o jẹ́ pe o ṣọ̀tọ́.

(13) Tí ó bá ri kin ní kan ba yì, tí o sì sọ wípé kí a wá ṣe. Eni naa lè sọ wípé jẹ́ kí a wa dan wò boya yio ṣeéṣe. Tí kò bá dè ṣeéṣe a a sọ pé kin ni yi kò ṣeéṣe, ṣùgbọ́n knan tí a sọ pé o ṣeéṣe ni ohun ti dawole ti o ṣeéṣe ni.

(14) Wọn lè la ye ara won ipe nkan tí o sọ wípé o mọ̀ yi tani ṣee lójú rẹ. Tí o ba sọ wípé ni ọjọ́ yẹn oun pẹ̀lú ẹni bayi ni ó jókò.

(15) Ọ̀nà tí a lè gbà wípé, a o bí ẹnikínní wípé kin ni ó ri kí o to sọ èyí, a ṣe àlàyé ye ọ, kin ni iwọ náà rí kí o tó má gbà àlàyé?

(16) Mo so wípé ọ̀jọ̀ yi nkù tí mo gbọ́ à ní iró ni pé kò kù. Ki a maa jiyàn lórí èyí. Kí ẹnikẹta wá sọ pé ọ̀jọ̀ kọ́ pé mọ́tò kan ni, ṣé o ri wípé ẹlẹ́kẹta yí ti yan jù ọ̀rọ̀.

(17) Tí ẹni yẹn bá sì jẹ́ ẹ̀rí tìí, ẹni tí ó njiyàn sọ wípé òun gbàgbọ́.

(18) Ki eni kan sọ wípé òun rí yin tí ẹ njó ṣùgbọ́n kí ẹnikejì tún so wípé òun rí ẹnikan tì o njo ṣùgbọ́n ẹyin kò ri ẹni tí oun rí.

Ó gbàgbé ni, kí a gbà pé kò fi ojú dá nkan. Bi ẹni yẹn kò bá gbà, kí ó sọ wípé nkan tí òun rí gan nìyẹn.

Bí ẹnikẹta bá ti wà níbíyìíó sọ wípé òótọ́ ni ẹni yẹn sọ, a sọ wípé ni ko sọ ojú da.

Njẹ́ kò ṣeéṣe kí àwọn méjéèjí mọ̀ dájú kí wọn gbà pé ẹyin ni wọn rí.

Bẹ́ẹ̀ni, á jẹ́ wípé ẹ̀mi wọn ṣiṣẹ́ pọ̀. Njẹ́ kò ṣeéṣe náà kí àwọn méèjí sọ wípé òun ni nkan tí wọn rí?

Kò ṣeéṣe.

(19) O lè bèèrè wípé ṣé o gbà kí nwá tàbí kí nma wà mo lè sọ wípé mo gbà, èyí ni pé o témi lọ́rùn.

(20) Kí ẹnikan ṣe nkan, kí won sì bèèrè lọ́wọ́ mi kí nsọ wípé mo ti gbọ́. Èyí jás wípé ó ti sọ fún mi.

(21) Nkan tí a fi ojú ara eni rí, nkan tí ènìyàn rí pátá. Kò kì nṣe nkan tí wọn sọ fún ènìyàn. Ṣé nkan tí wọn sọ fún ènìyàn kò yé ni bóyá irọ́ ni tàbí òótọ́ ni, ṣùgbọ́n tí ọ bá ti fi ojú kan báyìí yio ti yé ọ pé mo ti fi ojú ara mi rí kin ní náà.

(22) Tí a bá ti nwo ìwà ènìyàn, a lè sọ wípé a gbà wípé ó lè ṣé, tí kò bá tí ì ṣe nkan yẹn lójú rẹ̀, yìò wá sọ wípé òun mọ èyí ni pé èyí ti dá lójú.

(23) Èyí ni pé kò jẹ́ ẹ ni ẹ̀rí ọkọ̀n òun ni ẹ̀rí ọkọ̀n kò jẹ.

(24) Nígbàtí òyìnbó sọ pé òun nlo sí ilé mi nísisiyìí, ṣé kò mọ̀ pé mo wà nílé, kí ó mà sì mọ̀ pé emi rí òun, kí ó wá padà, kí nwá padà ri kí nsì bèèrè pé njẹ́ o ti wá síbí nísiyìí kí ó sọ wípé òun kò wá, kí a sọ títí kí ó tó gbà pé òun wá. Tàbí kí nbèèrè lógbólóhùn kan kí ó sọ wípé òun kò wá. 'Òun wá' yẹn ni èmi yio gbàgbọ́, jù wípé òun kò wá.

(25) Èyí ni pé, ó nrí bí ẹniyìí ṣe kiní yìí, ṣùgbọ́n kò ri pé o ṣé. Ó dá mi lójú, èyí ni pé mo ri òótọ́ ni ó ṣé kin ni yìí, ó ti dá ẹ lójú ni.

(26) Ṣùgbọ́n bí o bá ti nṣe elékèé ẹnikẹ́ni kò ní gbàgbọ́ wọn a sọ pé ó purọ́ wọn kò ní dáhùn si.

(27) Èyí ni nkan tí ẹ̀nì yìí kó ṣe tí wọn so wípé ó ṣe. A sọ wípé irọ́ ni wọn pa.

(28) Nígbàtí a sọ̀rọ̀ lana yẹn, tí mo sọ pé kí ẹ wá loni yẹn ẹ gbàgbọ́, ṣùgbọ́n kí ntún wá sọ wípé mo ti sọ pé kí ẹ wá, ṣùgbọ̀n bóyá ẹ kò ní wá eyì jẹ́ iyè méjì. Ṣùgbọ́n bí èyin ṣe wá yìi tí èmi náà dẹ wà yí, a jijọ ní igbàgbọ́. Oníyèmejì ni kò nro nkan tí ó sọ lána, ó ṣeéṣe kí ó má fi nkan tí ó so l'aná ṣẹ.

(29) Eyí ni a wípé oníjèméyì, kò ní igbàgbọ́.

(30) Ìgbàtí o bá rí ohun tí ọkọ̀n rẹ sọ. Tí o sì nṣe iyè mèjì.

(31) Bí o bá di nkan yìí mú, kí o dì mú síbẹ̀, ma fi sílẹ̀ kí o di òmíràn mú, o lè fi sílẹ̀ kí o di òmíràn mú. Òun ni Ọlọ́run fi sọ wípé kí a bèrè igbàgbọ́ lái se iyè méjì. Bí ọkàn ènìyàn bá ti nlọ báyìí tí o nlọ bayìí oníyèméjì kò lè rí nkan kan gbà lọ́wọ́ Ọlọ́run.

(32) Bí ènìyàn bá nsọ nkan bi o bá ti lọ sọ bí ọ́rọ̀ ẹranko. Tàbí ọ̀rọ̀ agọ̀ igbá yẹn ni awọn ènìyàn a wá sọ pé 'ẹ i ṣi bẹ́ẹ̀ kán àn wí', báyìí ni àwọn ènìyàn nwí. Tí o bá ṣe ènìyàn gidigidi yìò mọ̀ pé nkan tí o sọ nígbà yẹn kò dára.

(33) Tí èmi ẹnikan kò bá dúró lórí nkan tí ó nkọ, tí etí yìí tilẹ̀ ngbọ́ kò ni yée. Ṣé o mọ̀ wípé ọkọ̀n ni ígbọ́ran wà. Gbogbo ohun tí ó bá nkọ́ ni báyìí tí o bá ti nfi etí gbọ́ ó nlọ ọ sọ́kàn.

(34) Àwa náà itàn ni a lè gbọ́, a o sọ wípé àwọ́n baba wa ti sọ wípé irú nkan yìí ti ṣẹlẹ̀ rí, ṣùgbọ́n àwọn tí ó ti kú kò lè padà wá mo nkan yìí. À kò lè mọ nkan tí nwon ti se ní àtijọ́. Ṣùgbọ́n àwọ́n tí ó ti kú ko lè wá mọ nkan tí onṣe báyìí . . . Èyì tí o fi ojú rí yẹn ni o máa gbàgbọ́ jù.

(35) Èyí ni a npè ní àgbọ́sọ, nkan tí wọn kò wí ní ojú rẹ tí o sì wá nsọ, ṣùgbọ́n tí ènìyàn kò bá ti gbọ́ fún ra rẹ̀ yìò máa sọ.

(36) Mo sọ wípé bẹ̀ẹ̀ lá a rí, á jẹ́ wípé ọ̀rọ̀ àgbà ṣẹ ó jẹ́ à sọ tẹ́lẹ̀.

145

(37) Nkan tí kò yẹ ọ, ṣùgbọ́n o gbọ́. Ṣùgbọ́n igbà tí o kò ríi, ṣùgbọ́n o gbọ́.

(38) Ò jẹ ọ̀rọ̀ àbínibí, ó jẹ nkan tí baba mi nsọ lójú mi.

(39) Tí ó bá ti jẹ́ eni tí o ntùnpinpin ọ̀rọ̀, tí ó nbéèrè ọ̀rọ̀ l'ọ́wọ́ ẹni, ó lè bẹ̀ẹ̀rẹ̀ l'ọ́wọ́ eni mẹ́ta mẹ́rin tí yíò máa sọ fún ọ, iwó yíò mọ̀ọ́ ju ẹni tí ó dákẹ́, bí o tilẹ̀ rí báyìí tí kò ṣọ̀rọ̀. Nínú ẹni mẹ́ta mẹ́rin nì, wọn lè máa sọ ohun kan tàbí méjì fún ọ, nínú ohun kan tàbí méjì ni, ọjọ́ tí ẹnikẹ́ni bá ti béèrè wá a rí èyí tí o ba jọ níbẹ̀.

(40) Èí ni imọ̀ ifọkọ̀nsí gan tí ẹ lọ nkọ́ ní ilé ẹ̀kọ́ ṣé o ri pé olùkọ́ yin ko ki nbá yin wá sílé. Tí ẹ bá délé e ógbé iwé pé báyìí báyìí ni a kọ́ lóni, èyí dábi enipé báyìí bayìí ni baba wa ti wì–ifọkán sí ni.

(41) Tí wọn bá ti kọ́ ènìyàn ní oògùn tàbí bí wọn bá pa ìtàn fún ènìyàn wọn a fi sínú, inu ni ó ngbé, ohun tí wọn bá npa ní ìtàn fún ènìyàn nísisiyìí, wọn á máa fi sí inú iwé ni. Yío dẹ̀ yè síbẹ̀ láéláé ko ni si wípé ènìyàn míràn tún un pá ní ọjọ́ míràn ṣùgbọ́n kí o gbé iwé yẹn kí o dẹ̀ máakàà.

(42) Tí ènìyàn bá bí ọmọ rẹ a máa kọ lọ́gbọ́n, tí bàbá yẹn bá dàgbà a má a sọ wípé báyìí báyìí ni wọn ti se sọọ́ fún mi.

(43) Èyí ni npè ní òyé, tí ènìyàn bá ti ní àgbà síwájú tí ó bá nsọ̀rọ̀ tí wọn ti sọ níwájú rẹ̀ lọ́dún márun tàbí lọ́dún mẹ́wa, wọn á sọ wípé 'ọmọdé yìí mà lóye púpọ́'. Òyé òun ní a npè lógbọ́n àti àigbàgbé àti làákàyè–nkan tí a nfi nrántí nkan tí a ti ṣe.

(44) Kí àwa mẹ́rin máa sòrọ̀ kí ẹníkínní sọ pé òun gbà, kí èkejì sọ wípé òun gbà ṣùgbọ́n kí ènìyàn kan má gbà a o sọ pé kín nin ṣe tí iwọ kò fara mọ ọ̀rọ̀ yìí, kí gbogbo wa ṣe iwàasu si kí ó wá sọ pé òun gbà, tí gbogbo wa bá gbà tán a ó sọ wípé ọ̀rọ̀ yẹn ti papọ̀, ṣùgbọ́n kò papọ̀ nígbàtí àwọn kan gbà tí àwọn kan kò gbà.

(45) Èyí wà ní àríyàn jiyàn. Wọ́n lè sọ wípé kí wọn ma ṣe sọ dìjà pé kí wọn lọ wá'dìí rẹ̀.

(46) Tí mo bá nbá ènìyàn nrin, ma mọ gbogbo iwà rẹ̀, èyí tí ó lè ṣe àti èyí tí o kò lèṣé. Tí ẹnikan wá sọ fún mi pé o ṣe kinní kan báyìí, níwọ̀n igbàtí ó jẹ́ pé mo ti mọ iwà rẹ, tí ó bá ṣe pé o kò ṣé, èmi yí ó gbà ó gbọ́ pé o kò ṣé, ṣùgbọ́n bí iwà rẹ kò bá yé mi, tí o nṣe ségeṣège, mà a sọ wípé èmi kò mọ iwà rẹ pé èmi kò gbàgbọ́ pé o kò lè ṣé.

(47) Mo gbà ọ́ gbọ́ níbgà tí mo rí iwà rẹ, èyí tí o rí yẹn ni ó jù, mo ri dájúdájú. Mo gbà ọ gbọ́ ṣùgbọ́n èmi kò rí nkan náà, ṣùgbọ́n èyí tí mo rí kedere yẹn ni ó dájú.

(48) Tí wọn bá sọ wípé ẹnì kan ṣe nkan tí ó sì dá ẹnikéjì lójú pé kò lè ṣe irú nkan béè a lè sọ pé mo gbàgbọ́ tàbí mo gba eni yẹn gbọ́ kò lè ṣe irú nkan bẹ́ẹ̀. Tàbí kí ó sọ wípé mo gbàbgọ́ pé o lè ṣè é, èyí ni pé o ti mọ àdìn rẹ̀.

(49) Ìyàtọ̀ tí ó wà láàrín nkan tí mo mọ̀ àti èyí tí mo gbà ni pé, nkan tí o jẹ́ ki o gbà ni ó jẹ́ wípé o ti rí nkan náà, tàbí wípé lágbájá kò npurọ́ ló jẹ́ kí a gbà.

146

(50) Kí ọ̀rọ̀ kan wà nílẹ̀, kí o wá sọ fún mi, kí o sọ gbogbo rẹ̀ 'gbuuru', tí kò bá yé mí dáadáa èmi á wá sọ wípé ṣe àlàyé iṣe tí ọ̀rọ̀ yìi ṣe bẹ̀rẹ̀. Ìgbà yẹn ni iwọ náà yio wá sọ lẹ́sẹ̀ẹsẹ̀. Tí ó bá ṣe iṣẹ́ ni o bẹ̀ mí igbà yẹn ni yío wá yé mí.

(51) Àlàyè burúkú wà. Tí nba fẹ́ tàn ọ́ jẹ, èmi yí o ṣe àlàyé burúkú fún ọ; tí nkò bá fẹ́ tàn ọ́ jẹ èmí yí o ṣe àlàyé tí ó dára fún ọ. Nkan tí ó dára ni máa fi yé ọ, á jẹ́ wípé mo fẹ́ràn rẹ. Tí nbá fẹ́ tàn ọ, àlàyé tí mo máa ṣe fún ọ kò ní dára, ṣé kò ní mọ̀ wípé ọ̀nà tí mo fi síwájú rẹ̀ kò dára, oríṣi méjì yẹn ni àlàyé.

(52) Èyí ti bọ́ sí iyàn jíjà. Bí o bá nwádìí ọ̀rọ̀ tí ọ̀rọ̀ ẹni mẹ́ta bára mu, tí ti ẹni méjì yàtọ̀ tí mẹ́ta kò yàtọ̀, ṣùgbọ́n kí a pe gbogbo wọn pọ̀ láti wá maa sọ nkan tí wọn ti sọ, kí ọ̀kànkan nínú wọ́n má sọ nkan tí ó ti sọ tẹ́lẹ̀ a o sọ wípé ọ̀rọ̀ ná à ti papọ̀ kò ní yan jú mọ́, à fi kí a ní sùúrù kí a bẹ̀rẹ̀ idí míran wíwá.

(53) Tí ènìyàn bá bí ọmọ rẹ̀ a máa kọ lógbọ́n, tí bàbá yẹn bá dàgbà a má a sọ wípé báyìí báyìí ni wọn ti ṣe nṣọ́ọ́ fún mi. Nkan tí o ti ríríí à máa sọ fún ọmọ rẹ. Ṣé ọmọ rẹ kò rí kinní yẹn rí. Nkan tí a kò bá ríríí tí wọn sọ fún ọ, ni ó njẹ́ pé báyìbáyì ni wọn nsọ fún wa.

(54) . . . wàa sọ pé ó fi ojú ara rẹ ri pé òótọ́ ló dúró. Kò yẹ kí o ṣe iyè méjì.

Bibliography

(* indicates publications in which *KBW* or its antecedents are discussed)

ABIMBOLA, Wande. 1975. *Sixteen Great Poems of Ifa*. Zaria, Nigeria: UNESCO and Gaskiya Corporation.

————. 1976. *Ifa*. Oxford: Oxford University Press.

————. 1977. *Ifa Divination Poetry*. New York: NOK Publishers.

*ABIMBOLA, Wande, and HALLEN, Barry. 1993. 'Secrecy and Objectivity in the Methodology and Literature of Ifá Divination'. In M.H. NOOTER (ed.), *Secrecy: African Art That Conceals and Reveals*, New York: Museum for African Art, and Munich: Prestel, 213–221.

ABRAHAM, Karl. 1954. 'Contributions to the Theory of the Anal Character' and 'The Influence of Oral Eroticism on Character'. In *Selected Papers of Karl Abraham, M.D.* New York: Basic Books.

ABRAHAM, R.C. 1958. *Dictionary of Modern Yoruba*. London: University of London Press.

ADLER, Alfred. 1965. *Understanding Human Nature*. Greenwich, Conn.: Fawcett Publications.

*APPIAH, K. Anthony. 1992. *In My Father's House: Africa in the Philosophy of Culture*. Oxford: Oxford University Press.

ARMSTRONG, D. 1973. *Belief, Truth, and Knowledge*. Cambridge: Cambridge University Press.

AUSTIN, J.L. 1961. *Philosophical Papers*. Oxford: Oxford University Press.

————. 1962a. *Sense and Sensibilia*. Oxford: Oxford University Press.

————. 1962b. *How to Do Things with Words*. Oxford: Oxford University Press.

BASCOM, William R. 1969. *The Yoruba of Southwestern Nigeria*. New York: Holt, Rinehart and Winston.

————. 1969. *Ifa Divination: Communication Between Gods and Man in West Africa*. Bloomington: Indiana University Press.

BEATTIE, John. 1966a. *Other Cultures*. London: Routledge and Kegan Paul.

————. 1966b. 'Ritual and Social Change'. *Man* (N.S.) 1: 60–74.

————. 1970. 'On Understanding Ritual'. In WILSON (ed.), *Rationality*, 240–268.

*BEDU-ADDO, J.T. 1983. 'Sense-Experience and Recollection in Plato's *Meno*'. *American Journal of Philology* 104: 228–248.

*BELLO, A.G.A. 1988. 'Review of *Knowledge, Belief, and Witchcraft*'. *Journal of African Philosophy and Studies* 1/1–2: 93–98.

*BODUNRIN, Peter. 1981. 'The Question of African Philosophy'. *Philosophy* 56: 161–179. Reprinted in WRIGHT (ed.), *African Philosophy*, 2–23.

BOLTON, D.E. 1979. 'Quine on Meaning and Translation'. *Philosophy* 54: 230–248.

BRADLEY, M.C. 1975. 'Kirk on Indeterminacy of Translation'. *Analysis* 36: 18–22.

BRANDT, R.B. 1959. *Ethical Theory*. Englewood Cliffs, N.J.: Prentice-Hall.

BUXTON, Jean. 1968. 'Animal Identity and Human Peril: Some Mandari Images'. *Man* (N.S.) 3: 35–49.

———. 1973. *Religion and Healing in Mandari*. Oxford: Oxford University Press.

*BYRNE, Peter. 1987. 'Review of *Knowledge, Belief, and Witchcraft*'. *Religion Today* 14/3: 6–7.

CHOMSKY, Noam. 1969. 'Quine's Empirical Assumptions'. *Synthèse* 19: 53–68.

CLIFFORD, James. 1988. *The Predicament of Culture: Twentieth-Century Ethnography, Literature, and Art*. Cambridge, Mass.: Harvard University Press.

CLIFFORD, James, and MARCUS, George. 1986. *Writing Culture: The Poetics and Politics of Ethnography*. Berkeley: University of California Press.

COOPER, David E. 1975. 'Alternative Logic in "Primitive Thought"'. *Man* (N.S.) 10: 238–256.

*CORDWELL, J.M. 1987. 'Review of *Knowledge, Belief, and Witchcraft*'. *African Arts* 20/2: 76–78.

DAVIDSON, Donald. 1974a. 'Belief and the Basis of Meaning'. *Synthèse* 27: 309–323.

———. 1974b. 'On the Very Idea of a Conceptual Scheme'. *Proceedings and Addresses of the American Philosophical Association* 47: 5–20.

DAVIDSON, Donald, et al. 1974. 'First General Discussion Session, Conference on Intentionality, Language and Translation'. *Synthèse* 27: 467–508.

DE CERTEAU, Michel. 1986. *Heterologies: Discourse on the Other*. Minneapolis: University of Minnesota Press.

DEVITT, M., and STERELNY, K. 1987. *Language and Reality: An Introduction to the Philosophy of Language*. Cambridge, Mass.: MIT Press.

A Dictionary of the Yoruba Language. 1950. (Originally the Church Missionary Society [CMS] dictionary.) Oxford: Oxford University Press.

DIETERLEN, Germain. 1951. *Essai sur la réligion bambara*. Paris: Presses Universitaires de France.

DOUGLAS, Mary. 1966. *Purity and Danger*. New York: Praeger.

DRETSKE, F. 1988. *Explaining Behavior*. Cambridge, Mass.: MIT Press.

DUERR, Hans Peter. 1985. *Dreamtime: Concerning the Boundary Between Wilderness and Civilization*. Oxford: Basil Blackwell.

DUMMETT, Michael. 1993. *The Seas of Language*. Oxford: Clarendon Press.

EVANS-PRITCHARD, E.E. 1937. *Witchcraft, Oracles and Magic Among the Azande*. Oxford: Oxford University Press.

———. 1956. *Nuer Religion*. Oxford: Oxford University Press.

EWEN, C. L'Estrange. 1971. *Witch Hunting and Witch Trials*. London: Frederick Muller.

FABIAN, Johannes. 1983. *Time and the Other: How Anthropology Makes Its Object*. New York: Columbia University Press.

———. 1986. *Language and Colonial Power*. Cambridge: Cambridge University Press.

——— (ed.). 1990a. *History from Below: The Vocabulary of Elisabethville*. Philadelphia: J. Benjamins.

———. 1990b. 'Presence and Representation: The Other and Anthropological Writing'. *Critical Inquiry* 16/4: 753–772.

———. 1995. 'Ethnographic Misunderstanding and the Perils of Context'. *American Anthropologist* 97/1: 41–50.

FAVRET-SAADA, Jeanne. 1980. *Deadly Words*. Cambridge: Cambridge University Press.

FETZER, James (ed.). 1991. *Epistemology and Cognition*. Boston: Kluwer Academic Publishers.

FEYERABEND, Paul. 1975. *Against Method: Outline of an Anarchistic Theory of Knowledge*. London: New Left Books.

FIRTH, R. 1966. 'Twins, Birds and Vegetables'. *Man* (N.S.) 1: 1–17.

FROMM, Erich. 1967. *Man for Himself*. Greenwich, Conn.: Fawcett Publications.

GATES, Henry Louis, Jr. 1986. *'Race', Writing, and Difference*. Chicago: University of Chicago Press.

———. 1988. *The Signifying Monkey: A Theory of Afro-American Literary Criticism*. Oxford: Oxford University Press.

GBADEGESIN, 'Segun. 1991. *African Philosophy: Traditional Yoruba Philosophy and Contemporary African Realities*. New York: Peter Lang.

GELLNER, Ernest. 1959. *Words and Things: An Examination of, and an Attack on, Linguistic Philosophy*. London: Routledge and Kegan Paul.

———. 1970. 'Concepts and Society'. In WILSON (ed.), *Rationality*, 18–49.

———. 1974. *Legitimation of Belief*. Cambridge: Cambridge University Press.

GOLDMAN, A. 1986. *Epistemology and Cognition*. Cambridge, Mass.: Harvard University Press.

GOODY, Jack. 1961. 'Religion and Ritual: The Definitional Problem'. *British Journal of Sociology* 12: 142–164.

———. 1977. *The Domestication of the Savage Mind*. Cambridge: Cambridge University Press.

———. 1987. *The Interface Between the Written and the Oral*. Cambridge: Cambridge University Press.

GOODY, J., and WATT, I. 1963. 'The Consequences of Literacy'. *Comparative Studies in Society and History* 5: 304–345. Reprinted in J. GOODY (ed.), *Literacy in Traditional Societies*, Cambridge: Cambridge University Press, 1968, 27–68.

GRIAULE, Marcel. 1965. *Conversations with Ogotemmeli*. Oxford: Oxford University Press.

GYEKYE, Kwame. 1987. *An Essay on African Philosophical Thought*. Cambridge: Cambridge University Press.

*HAACK, Susan. 1993. *Evidence and Inquiry: Towards Reconstruction in Epistemology*. Oxford: Basil Blackwell.

HABERMAS, Jürgen. 1987. *The Philosophical Discourse of Modernity: Twelve Lectures*. Cambridge, Mass.: MIT Press.

HACKING, Ian. 1973. *Why Does Language Matter to Philosophy?* Cambridge: Cambridge University Press.

*HALLEN, Barry. 1975. 'A Philosopher's Approach to Traditional Culture'. *Theoria to Theory* 9: 259–272.

———. 1976. 'Phenomenology and the Exposition of African Traditional Thought'. *Second Order* 5: 45–65. Reprinted in Claude SUMNER (ed.), *African Philosophy*, Addis Ababa: Chamber Printing House, 1980, 56–80.

*———. 1977. 'Robin Horton on Critical Philosophy and Traditional Thought'. *Second Order* 6: 81–92. Revised and reprinted as 'Analytic Philosophy and Traditional Thought: A Critique of Robin Horton', in P. ENGLISH and K.M. KALUMBA (eds.), *African Philosophy: A Classical Approach*, Englewood Cliffs, N.J.: Prentice-Hall, 1996, 216–228.

*———. 1979. 'The [African] Art Historian as Conceptual Analyst'. *Journal of Aesthetics and Art Criticism* 37: 303–313.

*———. 1981. 'The Open Texture of Oral Tradition'. *Theoria to Theory* 14: 327–332.

*———. 1985. 'Review of APOSTEL, L., and STORY, E., *African Philosophy: Myth or Reality*'. *Journal of the Philosophy of the Social Sciences* 15/1 (March): 109–111.

———. 1989. ' "*Enìyàn*": A Critical Analysis of the Yoruba Concepts of Person'. In C.S. MOMOH (ed.), *The Substance of African Philosophy*, Auchi, Nigeria: African Philosophy Projects, 328–354.

*———. 1995a. 'Some Observations About Philosophy, Postmodernism, and Art in African Studies'. *African Studies Review* 38/1 (April): 69–80.

*———. 1995b. 'Indeterminacy, Ethnophilosophy, Linguistic Philosophy, African Philosophy'. *Philosophy* 70/273 (July): 377–393. (Included as the Afterword to the present volume.)

*———. 1995c. ' "Philosophy" Doesn't Translate: Richard Rorty and Multiculturalism, Parts I and II'. *SAPINA* [Society for African Philosophy in North America] *Bulletin* 8/3 (July–December): 1–42.

———. 1995d. ' "My Mercedes Has Four Legs!" "Traditional" as an Attribute of African Equestrian Culture'. In Gigi PEZZOLI (ed.), *Horsemen of Africa: History, Iconography, Symbolism*, Milan: Centro Studi Archeologia Africana, 49–64.

*———. 1997a. 'African Meanings, Western Words'. *African Studies Review* 40/1 (April).

*———. 1997b. 'Does It Matter Whether Linguistic Philosophy Intersects Ethnophilosophy? A Reaction to Paulin Hountondji'. *APA Newsletter on Philosophy and International Cooperation* (Spring).

*HALLEN, B., and SODIPO, J. Olubi. 1986. *Knowledge, Belief, and Witchcraft: Analytic Experiments in African Philosophy*. London: Ethnographica Publishers.

*———. 1994. 'The House of the *"Inú"*: Keys to a Yoruba Theory of the "Self" '. *Quest: Philosophical Discussions* 8/1: 3–23.

HALLPIKE, C.R. 1979. *The Foundations of Primitive Thought*. Oxford: Oxford University Press.

HARMAN, Gilbert. 1969. 'An Introduction to "Translation and Meaning": Chapter Two of *Word and Object*'. *Synthèse* 19: 14–26.

HAYLEY, Audrey. 1968. 'Symbolic Equations: The Ox and the Cucumber'. *Man* (N.S.) 3: 262–271.

HINTIKKA, Jaakko. 1969. 'Behavioural Criteria of Radical Translation'. *Synthèse* 19: 69–81.

HOBSBAWM, Eric, and RANGER, Terence (eds.). 1983. *The Invention of Tradition*. Cambridge: Cambridge University Press.

HOGAN, Robert. 1976. *Personality Theory*. Englewood Cliffs, N.J.: Prentice-Hall.

HOLLIS, Martin. 1970. 'The Limits of Irrationality'. In WILSON (ed.), *Rationality*, 214–220.

HOLLIS, Martin, and LUKES, Steven (eds.). 1982. *Rationality and Relativism*. Cambridge, Mass.: MIT Press.

HORTON, Robin. 1960. 'A Definition of Religion and Its Uses'. *Journal of the Royal Anthropological Institute* 90: 201–226.

———. 1967. 'African Traditional Thought and Western Science'. *Africa* 37: 50–71 and 155–187.

*———. 1982. 'Tradition and Modernity Revisited'. In HOLLIS and LUKES (eds.), *Rationality and Relativism*, 201–260.

*———. 1993. *Patterns of Thought in Africa and the West: Essays on Magic, Religion and Science*. Cambridge: Cambridge University Press.

*———. (n.d.) 'Traditional Thought and the Emerging African Philosophy Department: A Reply to Dr. Hallen'. Unpublished paper.

HORTON, Robin, and FINNEGAN, Ruth (eds.). 1973. *Modes of Thought*. London: Faber and Faber.

HOUNTONDJI, Paulin. 1983. *African Philosophy: Myth and Reality*. Bloomington: Indiana University Press.

———. 1985. 'The Pitfalls of Being Different'. *Diogenes* 131 (Fall): 46–56.

———. 1990. 'Scientific Dependence in Africa Today'. *Research in African Literatures* 21/3: 5–15.

———. 1995. 'Producing Knowledge in Africa Today'. *African Studies Review* 38/3: 1–10.

IRELE, Abiola. 1983. 'Introduction,' in HOUNTONDJI, *African Philosophy*, 7–30.

*JACKSON, Michael. 1989. *Paths Toward a Clearing: Radical Empiricism and Ethnographic Inquiry*. Bloomington: Indiana University Press.

JAMESON, Fredric. 1988. *The Ideologies of Theory: Essays 1971–1986*, Vol. 2, *Syntax and History*. Minneapolis: University of Minnesota Press.

JARVIE, I.C., and AGASSI, J. 1970. 'The Problem of the Rationality of Magic'. In WILSON (ed.), *Rationality*, 172–193.

*JORION, Paul. 1987. 'Review of *Knowledge, Belief, and Witchcraft*'. *L'Homme: Revue française d'anthropologie* 27/101: 160–162.

JUNG, Carl. 1966. 'On the Psychology of the Unconscious'. In *The Collected Works of C.G. Jung*, ed. H. Read, M. Fordham, and G. Adler, 7:1–201. Princeton, N.J.: Princeton University Press.

KAGAME, Alexis. 1956. *La Philosophie bantou-rwandaise de l'être*. Brussels: Mémoire in 8° de Académie Royale des Sciences Coloniales (N.S.) 12/1.

KATZ, J.J. 1988. 'The Refutation of Indeterminacy'. *Journal of Philosophy* 85/6 (May): 227–252.

KATZ, J.J., and FODOR, J. 1962. 'What's Wrong with the Philosophy of Language?' *Inquiry* 5/3: 197–237.

KIEV, Ari. 1969. 'The Study of Folk Psychiatry'. In Ari KIEV (ed.), *Magic, Faith, and Healing*. New York: Free Press, 3–35.

KIRK, Robert. 1986. *Translation Determined*. Oxford: Clarendon Press.

KUHN, Thomas. 1962. *The Structure of Scientific Revolutions*, 2nd ed. Chicago: University of Chicago Press.

LAITIN, David. 1977. *Politics, Language, and Thought*. Chicago: University of Chicago Press.

*———. 1986. *Hegemony and Culture: Politics and Religious Change Among the Yoruba*. Chicago: University of Chicago Press.

LAWSON, E.T., and MCCAULEY, R.N. 1990. *Rethinking Religion: Connecting Cognition and Culture*. Cambridge: Cambridge University Press.

LEHRER, Keith. 1974. *Knowledge*. Oxford: Oxford University Press.

LE PAGE, R.B., and TABOURET-KELLER, A. 1985. *Acts of Identity: Creole-Bases Approaches to Language and Ethnicity*. Cambridge: Cambridge University Press.

*LITHOWN, Robert. 1976. 'Barry Hallen on Philosophy and Traditional Culture'. *Theoria to Theory* 10: 161–166.

LUKES, Steven. 1970. 'Some Problems About Rationality'. In WILSON (ed.), *Rationality*, 194–213.

———. 1973. 'On the Social Determination of Truth'. In HORTON and FINNEGAN (eds.), *Modes of Thought*, 230–248.

LYOTARD, Jean-François. 1988. *The Postmodern Condition: A Report on Knowledge*. Minneapolis: University of Minnesota Press.

MACINTYRE, Alasdair. 1966. *A Short History of Ethics*. New York: Macmillan.

————. 1970. 'Is Understanding Religion Compatible with Believing?' In WILSON (ed.), *Rationality*, 62–77.

MAIR, Lucy. 1969. *Witchcraft*. London: Weidenfeld and Nicolson.

MARCUS, George (ed.). 1992. *Rereading Cultural Anthropology*. Durham, N.C.: Duke University Press.

MARCUS, G., and MYERS, F. (eds.). 1995. *The Traffic in Culture: Refiguring Art and Anthropology*. Berkeley: University of California Press.

MARWICK, M.G. 1973. 'How Real Is the Charmed Circle in African and Western Thought?' *Africa* 1: 59–70.

*MASOLO, D.A. 1994. *African Philosophy in Search of Identity*. Bloomington: Indiana University Press.

MCCLEAN, D.E. 1994. 'Afrocentrism as a Humanism—Difficulties of Popular Afrocentrism'. *APA Newsletters* 93/1 (Spring): 13–15.

*MOMOH, Campbell S. 1985. 'African Philosophy . . . Does It Exist?' *Diogenes* 130 (Summer): 73–104.

*MUDIMBE, V.Y. 1987. 'Review of *Knowledge, Belief, and Witchcraft*'. *Canadian Philosophical Reviews* 7/5: 200–202.

*————. 1988. *The Invention of Africa: Gnosis, Philosophy, and the Order of Knowledge*. Bloomington: Indiana University Press.

————. 1994. *The Idea of Africa*. Bloomington: Indiana University Press.

*MUDIMBE, V.Y., and APPIAH, K.A. 1993. 'The Impact of African Studies on Philosophy'. In R.H. BATES, V.Y. MUDIMBE, and J. O'BARR (eds.), *Africa and the Disciplines: The Contributions of Research in Africa to the Social Sciences and Humanities*, Chicago: University of Chicago Press, 113–138.

MILNER, G.B. 1969. 'Siamese Twins, Birds and the Double Helix'. *Man* (N.S.) 4: 5–23.

NEEDHAM, Rodney. 1972. *Belief, Language and Experience*. Oxford: Basil Blackwell.

NERLICH, Graham. 1976. 'Quine's "Real Ground" '. *Analysis* (N.S.) 37: 15–19.

NEWTON-SMITH, W. 1982. 'Relativism and the Possibility of Interpretation'. In HOLLIS and LUKES (eds.), *Rationality and Relativism*, 106–122.

NGUGI WA THIONG'O. 1985. 'The Language of African Literature'. *New Left Review* 150: 109–127.

*OKE, Moses. 1995. 'Towards an African (Yoruba) Perspective on Empirical Knowledge: A Critique of Hallen and Sodipo'. *International Philosophical Quarterly* 35/2 (June): 205–216.

OLUWOLE, Sophie. 1978. 'On the Existence of Witches'. *Second Order* 2: 20–35. Reprinted in A.G. MOSLEY (ed.), *African Philosophy: Selected Readings*, New York: Prentice-Hall, 1995, 357–370.

ONG, W.J. 1982. *Orality and Literacy: The Technologizing of the Word*. London and New York: Methuen.

*ORUKA, H.O. (ed.). 1990. *Sage Philosophy: Indigenous Thinkers and the Modern Debate on African Philosophy*. Leiden: E.J. Brill.

*OSEGHARE, A.S. 1992. 'Sagacity and African Philosophy'. *International Philosophical Quarterly* 32/1: 95–103.

OVERING, J. 1987. 'Translation as a Creative Process: The Power of the Name'. In L. HOLY (ed.), *Comparative Anthropology*, Oxford: Basil Blackwell, 70–87.

*OWOMOYELA, O. 1987. 'Africa and the Imperative of Philosophy: A Sceptical Consideration'. *African Studies Review* 30/1 (March): 79–99.

PARRINDER, Geoffrey. 1970. *Witchcraft: European and African*. London: Faber and Faber.

PEARCE, Carol. 1992. 'African Philosophy and the Sociological Thesis'. *Journal of the Philosophy of the Social Sciences* 22/4 (December): 440–460.

PECHEUX, Michel. 1982. *Language, Semantics, and Ideology*. New York: St. Martin's Press.

*PEEK, Philip. 1991. *African Divination Systems: Ways of Knowing*. Bloomington: Indiana University Press.

———. 1994. 'The Sounds of Silence: Cross-World Communication and the Auditory Arts in African Societies'. *American Ethnologist* 21/3: 474–494.

PEEL, J.D.Y. 1969. 'Understanding Alien Thought Systems'. *British Journal of Sociology* 20: 69–84.

POPPER, Karl. 1962. *Conjectures and Refutations: The Growth of Scientific Knowledge*. New York: Basic Books.

PRATT, Vernon. 1972. 'Science and Traditional African Religion'. *Second Order* 1: 7–20.

PRICE, H.H. 1969. *Belief*. London: George Allen and Unwin.

QUINE, W.V.O. 1953. 'Two Dogmas of Empiricism'. In *From a Logical Point of View*, Cambridge, Mass.: Harvard University Press, 20–46.

———. 1959. 'Meaning and Translation'. In J.A. FODOR and J.J. KATZ (eds.), *The Structure of Language*, Englewood Cliffs, N.J.: Prentice-Hall, 460–478.

———. 1960. *Word and Object*. Cambridge, Mass.: MIT Press.

———. 1968. 'Propositional Objects'. *Critica* 2: 3–22.

———. 1969a. 'Epistemology Naturalized'. In Department of Philosophy, Columbia University (ed.), *Ontological Relativity and Other Essays*, New York: Columbia University Press, 69–90.

———. 1969b. 'Existence and Quantification'. In *Ontological Relativity and Other Essays*, 91–113.

———. 1969c. 'Ontological Relativity'. In *Ontological Relativity and Other Essays*, 26–68.

———. 1969d. 'Speaking of Objects'. In *Ontological Relativity and Other Essays*, 1–25.

———. 1969e. 'Replies to: (1) HARMAN; (2) STENIUS; (3) CHOMSKY; (4) HINTIKKA; (5) STROUD'. *Synthèse* 19: 267–291.

————. 1969f. 'A Symposium on Austin's Method, II'. In K.T. FANN (ed.), *Symposium on J.L. Austin*, London: Routledge and Kegan Paul, 86–90.

————. 1969g. 'Linguistics and Philosophy'. In S. HOOK (ed.), *Language and Philosophy*, New York: New York University Press, and London: University of London Press, 95–98.

————. 1970a. *Philosophy of Logic*. Englewood Cliffs, N.J.: Prentice-Hall.

————. 1970b. 'On the Reasons for Indeterminacy of Translation'. *Journal of Philosophy* 68/6 (March): 178–183.

————. 1974. 'Comment on Donald Davidson'. *Synthèse* 27: 325–329.

————. 1975a. 'The Nature of Natural Knowledge'. In S. GUTTENPLAN (ed.), *Mind and Language*, Oxford: Oxford University Press, 67–81.

————. 1975b. 'Mind and Verbal Dispositions'. In GUTTENPLAN (ed.), *Mind and Language*, 83–95.

————. 1976. 'Quantifiers and Propositional Attitudes'. In *The Ways of Paradox and Other Essays*, Cambridge, Mass.: Harvard University Press, 183–194.

————. 1987. 'Indeterminacy of Translation Again'. *Journal of Philosophy* 84/1 (January): 5–10.

————. 1990a. 'Phoneme's Long Shadow'. In T. HEADLAND, K. PIKE, and M. HARRIS (eds.), *Emics and Etics: The Insider/Outsider Debate* (Frontiers of Anthropology, vol. 7), Newbury Park, Calif.: Sage Publications, 164–167.

————. 1990b. *The Pursuit of Truth*. Cambridge, Mass.: Harvard University Press.

————. 1993. 'In Praise of Observation Sentences'. *Journal of Philosophy* 90/3 (March): 107–116.

————. 1994a. 'Response to Abel'. *Inquiry* 37/4 (December): 495–496.

————. 1994b. 'Response to Davidson', *Inquiry* 37/4 (December): 498–500.

————. 1996. 'Progress on Two Fronts'. *Journal of Philosophy* 93/4 (April): 159–163.

QUINE, W.V.O., and ULLIAN, J.S. 1970. *The Web of Belief*. New York: Random House.

REYNOLDS, Vernon. 1973. 'Man Also Behaves'. In J. BENTHALL (ed.), *The Limits of Human Nature*, London: Allen Lane, 143–157.

*RIGBY, Peter. 1992. 'Practical Ideology and Ideological Practice: On African Episteme and Marxian Problematic — Ilparakuyo Maasai Transformations'. In V.Y. MUDIMBE (ed.), *The Surreptitious Speech: Présence Africaine and the Politics of Otherness 1947–1987*, Chicago: University of Chicago Press, 257–300.

RISJORD, Mark. 1993. 'Wittgenstein's Woodcutters: The Problem of Apparent Irrationality'. *American Philosophical Quarterly* 30/3 (July): 247–258.

RORTY, Richard. 1967. *The Linguistic Turn: Essays in Philosophical Method*. Chicago: University of Chicago Press, 1992.

RUSSELL, Bertrand. 1940. *An Inquiry into Meaning and Truth*. New York: Norton.

SALEMOHAMED, G. 1983. 'African Philosophy'. *Philosophy* 58/226 (October): 535–538.

SENGHOR, Leopold. 1964. *Liberté I: Négritude et humanisme*. Paris: Seuil.

SKORUPSKI, John. 1976. *Symbol and Theory*. Cambridge: Cambridge University Press.

SMART, J.J.C. 1969. 'Quine's Philosophy of Science'. *Synthèse* 19: 3–13.

*SODIPO, J. Olubi. 1973. 'Notes on the Concept of Cause and Chance in Yoruba Traditional Thought'. *Second Order* 2 (1973): 12–20.

*———. 1975. 'Philosophy in Africa Today'. *Thought and Practice* 2/2.

*———. 1983. 'Philosophy, Science, Technology and Traditional African Thought'. In H. O. ORUKA (ed.), *Philosophy and Cultures*, Nairobi: Bookwise, 36–43.

*———. 1984. 'Philosophy in Pre-Colonial Africa'. In *Teaching and Research in Philosophy: Africa*, Paris: UNESCO, 73–80.

*SOGOLO, G.S. 1993. *Foundations of African Philosophy: A Definitive Analysis of Conceptual Issues in African Thought*. Ibadan, Nigeria: Ibadan University Press.

SOYINKA, Wole. 1976. *Myth, Literature and the African World*. Cambridge: Cambridge University Press.

STICH, Stephen. 1983. *From Folk Psychology to Cognitive Science*. Cambridge, Mass.: MIT Press.

*———. 1987. 'Review of *Knowledge, Belief, and Witchcraft*'. *Ethics* 98/1 (October): 203.

*———. 1990. *The Fragmentation of Reason: Preface to a Pragmatic Theory of Cognitive Evaluation*. Cambridge, Mass.: MIT Press.

STRAWSON, Peter. 1959. *Individuals*. London: Routledge and Kegan Paul.

STROUD, Barry. 1969. 'Conventionalism and the Indeterminacy of Translation'. *Synthèse* 19: 82–96.

———. 1984. *The Significance of Philosophical Scepticism*. Oxford: Clarendon Press.

SUMMERS, Montague. 1973. *The History of Witchcraft and Demonology*. London: Routledge and Kegan Paul.

TAIWO, Olufemi. 1995. 'Appropriating Africa: An Essay on New Africanist Schools'. *Issue: A Journal of Opinion* [African Studies Association] 23/1: 39–45.

TAMBIAH, Stanley J. 1990. *Magic, Science, Religion, and the Scope of Rationality*. Cambridge: Cambridge University Press.

TEMPELS, Placide. 1959. *Bantu Philosophy*. Paris: Présence Africaine.

THOMAS, Keith. 1973. *Religion and the Decline of Magic*. Harmondsworth: Penguin Books.

TURNER, Victor. 1967. *The Forest of Symbols*. Ithaca, N.Y.: Cornell University Press.

URMSON, J.O. 1969. 'A Symposium on Austin's Method, I'. In K.T. FANN (ed.), *Symposium on J.L. Austin*, London: Routledge and Kegan Paul, 76–85.

*VANSINA, Jan. 1984. *Art History in Africa: An Introduction to Method*. London: Longman.

————. 1985. *Oral Tradition as History*. London: James Currey.

WILSON, Bryan (ed.). 1970. *Rationality*. Oxford: Basil Blackwell.

WINCH, Peter, 1958. *The Idea of a Social Science*. London: Routledge and Kegan Paul.

————. 1964. 'Understanding a Primitive Society'. *American Philosophical Quarterly* 1. Reprinted in WILSON (ed.), *Rationality*, 78–111.

WIREDU, Kwasi. 1972. 'On an African Orientation in Philosophy'. *Second Order* 1: 3–13.

————. 1980. *Philosophy and an African Culture*. Cambridge: Cambridge University Press.

*————. 1992a. 'On Defining African Philosophy'. In H. NAGL-DOCEKAL and F.M. WIMMER (eds.), *Postkoloniales Philosophieren: Afrika*, Vienna/Munich: R. Oldenbourg Verlag, 40–62.

————. 1992b. 'Formulating Modern Thought in African Languages: Some Theoretical Considerations'. In MUDIMBE (ed.), *The Surreptitious Speech*, 301–332. Reprinted in WIREDU 1996, 81–104.

*————. 1992–93. 'African Philosophical Tradition: A Case Study of the Akan'. *Philosophical Forum* 24/1–3: 35–62. Reprinted in WIREDU 1996, 113–135.

————. 1993. 'Canons of Conceptualization'. *The Monist* 76/4 (October): 450–476.

————. 1995. 'Are There Cultural Universals?' *The Monist* 78/1 (January): 52–64. Reprinted in WIREDU 1996, 21–33.

————. 1996. *Cultural Universals and Particulars: An African Perspective*. Bloomington and Indianapolis: Indiana University Press.

WITTGENSTEIN, Ludwig. 1949. *Tractatus logico-philosophicus*. London: Routledge and Kegan Paul.

————. 1958. *Philosophical Investigations*. New York: Macmillan.

————. 1980. *Culture and Value*. Oxford: Basil Blackwell.

*WRIGHT, Richard A., Jr. (ed.) 1984. *African Philosophy: An Introduction*, 3rd ed. Washington, D.C.: University Press of America.

Index

Library of Congress Cataloging-in-Publication Data

Hallen, B.
    Knowledge, belief, and witchcraft : analytic experiments in
African philosophy / Barry Hallen and J.O. Sodipo ; with a new
foreword by W.V.O. Quine ; and a new afterword by Barry Hallen.
       p.   cm. — (Mestizo spaces = Espaces métissés)
    Originally published: Ethnographica, 1986.
    Includes bibliographical references and index.
    ISBN 0-8047-2822-4 (cloth : alk. paper). — ISBN 0-8047-2823-2
(pbk. : alk. paper)
    1. Philosophy, Yoruba. 2. Yoruba language—Semantics.
3. Witchcraft—Nigeria. 4. Knowledge, Theory of. 5. Belief and
doubt. 6. Philosophy, African. I. Sodipo, J. O. II. Title.
III. Series: Mestizo spaces.
B5619.N6H35 1997
199′.6—dc21   96-53559
                                            CIP